Hermetic Mas

THE BEGINNING OF MASONRY

AND

A U M

"THE LOST WORD"

Frank C. Higgins

ISBN 0-922802-12-2

The Beginning of Masonry

THE ancient Cosmic Science, of which Freemasonry is the modern survival, gives the date of its inception, as that at which the above "Cardinal Signs" commenced their reign, viz. 3995 B. C., commonly reckoned as 4000 B. C., which, added to the current year, gives us our Masonic date.

INDEX

Avant Propos

This is a very small essay concerning a very big subject. Volumes have been written upon the presumed connection of Freemasonry with that vague *gnosis* of the past, called "the Ancient Mysteries," but concerning the intimate nature of the teaching imparted to initiates, following upon the ceremonies of reception, of which classic writers have given us some notion, nothing remains to us but widely scattered symbols.

It has been the pleasant life-work of the writer to join together, as best he could, the scattered pieces of this stupendous "cut out" puzzle and reconstitute the ancient fabric in such a manner as would stand the test of scientific examination and deserves to live for the benefit of future generations of men and Masons. These papers have been written as an elementary course designed to arouse interest in a far deeper investigation of the whole subject.

Notwithstanding the designedly universal character of the craft, the externals of Freemasonry possess an altogether human tendency to become reflexes of the communities in which they flourish.

The re-nascent Masonic intellectual activity of the past few years, no more splendid example of which can be cited than the foundation and upbuilding of the National Masonic Research Society, throws strongly into relief the fact that our American Masonry, has, until quite recently, exerted little effort on other than social and fraternal lines. The wonderful development of Masonic benevolent institutions throughout the United States, has reflected the brotherhood and liberality of Masonic manhood, but it has been accomplished in the presence of an almost total oblivion of what was *once* the principal reason for the existence of Masonic associations.

This consisted in the enlightenment of those who were found worthy and well qualified to receive deeper insight into the philosophy of existence and hidden historical truths of a nature too disturbing of common acceptances to be spread broadcast among the masses. So, in the absence of fostering interest, American Masonry has been, little by little, so divested of all connection with the pursuit of the deeper Masonic significances, as to have become, on the side of progressive speculation, a pale shadow of the Old World Craft. The true philosophic mission of Masonry, such as was the original intention of the "symbolic" Lodge, no less than the Scottish Rite, could scarcely be better expressed, than in the

5

following translation from the Spanish, of a lecture intended for the edification of a foreign Lodge.

"Know, Brother, by that which has already been shewn you and may yet come to your knowledge through the enlightening medium of History, that in the days of antiquity, in India, in Persia, in Egypt and in Greece and Rome, the first initiates in the principles, designed in their purity to serve as the foundation of universal Masonry, especially the sacerdotal and other privileged classes, profiting by the knowledge gained and iniquitously turning awry the straight path of progress in understanding, instead of fulfilling a mission of noble civilization, mounted and grasping the reins of inordinate power, especially throughout the Eastern world, tyrannized over the Nations.

"Initiation, during the ages to which I refer, consisted in the communication of certain philosophical truths, of a Natural order, enabling man to profit by the productive periods of Mother Earth, who is prodigal of her fruits at certain epochs but at others displays herself less liberal, also in the imparting of certain liberal Arts, which gave special advantages to those who exercised them, while at the same time uplifting them spiritually.

"These truths, useful practices and elevating arts, at the cost of terrific struggles, sustained century after century, have finally become the patrimony of all mankind, with exception, perhaps, of the relatively few which, through various circumstances remain beyond the grasp of ordinary humanity.

"In the ages of which I speak, that which was most important, was a correct knowledge of the seasons of the year, with especial reference to the productiveness of the earth, and as there were no industries directed to the multiplication, cultivation and preservation of her gifts, this knowledge constituted the bread of the hungry and the daily food of entire peoples.

"Thus it was that astronomical notions were deified and that the Sun, observed as the genius of good and considered the Creator, in perpetual strife with the principles of Evil, residing in the mists and darkness supplied by the terrors of human imagination, became the origin of mythological allegories, more or less poetical in character, according to the varied spirituality of the races of mankind."

The following pages accommodate little more than a series of allusions, but it has been sought to render them sufficiently consecutive, to present a comprehensive picture, to the reader, of the ground over which he must travel in search of true Masonic origins and significances.

FRANK C. HIGGINS.

New York, October, 1916.

6

The First Books of Masonry

*A part of Victor Hugo's famous chapter, "This Will Destroy That,"
from his "Notre Dame de Paris," in which he elaborates upon the part
that architecture had in recording the knowledge of the ancients and
moderns down to the 15th century.*

From the very beginning of things down to the 15th century, architecture is the great book of the human race, man's chief means of expressing the various stages of his development, whether physical or mental.

When the memory of the primitive races began to be surcharged, when the load of tradition carried about by the human family grew so heavy and disordered that the Word, naked and fleeting, ran danger of being lost by the way, they transcribed it on the ground by the most visible, the most lasting, and at the same time most natural means. They inclosed each tradition in a monument.

The first monuments were simply squares of rock "which had not been touched by iron," as says Moses. Architecture began like all writing. It was first an alphabet. A stone was planted upright, and it was a letter, and each letter was a hieroglyph, and on every hieroglyph rested a group of ideas, like the capital on the column. Thus did the primitive races act at the same moment over the entire face of the globe. One finds the "upright stone" of the Celts in Asiatic Siberia and on the pampas of America.

Presently they constructed words. Stone was laid upon stone, these granite syllables were coupled together, the Word essayed some combinations. The Celtic *dolmen* and *cromlech*, the Etruscan *tumulus*, the Hebrew *gilgal*, are words; some of them, the *tumulus* in particular, are proper names. Occasionally, when there were many stones and a vast expanse of ground, they wrote a sentence. The immense mass of stones at Karnac is already a complete formula.

Last of all they made books. Traditions had ended by bringing forth symbols, under which they disappeared like the trunk of a tree under its foliage. These symbols, in which all humanity believed, continued to grow and multiply, becoming more and more complex.

Of necessity the symbol must expand into the edifice.

7

Architecture followed the development of human thought; it became a giant with a thousand heads, a thousand arms, and caught and concentrated in one eternal, visible, tangible form all this floating symbolism.

The parent idea, the Word, was contained not only in the foundation of these edifices, but in their structure. Solomon's Temple, for example, was not simply the cover of the sacred book: it was the sacred book itself. On each of its concentric inclosures the priest might read the Word translated and made manifest to the eye, might follow its transformation from sanctuary to sanctuary, till at last he could lay hold upon it in its final tabernacle, under its most concrete form, which yet was architecture,— the Ark. Thus the Word was inclosed in the edifice; but its image was visible on its outer covering, like the human figure depicted on the coffin of a mummy.

Thus during the first 6,000 years of the world—from the most immemorial temple of Hindustan to the Cathedral at Cologne—architecture has been the great manuscript of the human race. And this is true to such a degree that not only every religious symbol, but every human thought, has its page and its memorial in that vast book.

The reign of many masters succeeding the reign of one, is written in architecture. For—and this point we must emphasize—it must not be supposed that it is capable only of building temples, of expressing only the sacerdotal myth and symbolism, of transcribing in hieroglyphics on its stone pages the mysterious Tables of the Law. Were this the case, then— seeing that in every human society there comes a moment when the sacred symbol is worn out, and is obliterated by the free thought, when the man breaks away from the priest, when the growth of philosophies and systems eats away the face of religion—architecture would be unable to reproduce this new phase of the human mind: its leaves, written upon the right side, would be blank on the reverse; its work would be cut short; its book incomplete. But that is not the case.

This was the only form, however, in which free thought was possible, and therefore it found full expression only in those books called edifices. Under that form it might have looked on at its own burning at the hands of the common hangman had it been so imprudent as to venture into manuscript; the thought embodied in the church door would have assisted at the death agony of the thought expressed in the book. Therefore, having but this one outlet, it rushed toward it from all parts; and hence the countless mass of cathedrals spread over all Europe, a number so prodigious that it seems incredible, even after verifying it with one's own eyes. All the material, all the intellectual forces of society, converged to that one point,—architecture. In this way, under the pretext of building churches to the glory of God, the art developed to magnificent proportions.

Thus, till Gutenberg's time, architecture is the chief, the universal, form of writing; in this stone book, begun by the East, continued by Ancient Greece and Rome, the Middle Ages have written the last page. For the rest, this phenomenon of an architecture belonging to the people, succeeding an architecture belonging to a caste, which we have observed in the Middle Ages, occurs in precisely analogous stages in human intelligence at other great epochs of history. Thus—to sum up here in a few lines a law which would call for volumes to do it justice—in the Far East, the cradle of primitive history, after Hindu architecture comes the Phenician, that fruitful mother of Arabian architecture; in antiquity, Egyptian architecture, of which the Etruscan style and the Cyclopean monuments are but a variety, is succeeded by the Greek, of which the Roman is merely a prolongation burdened with the Carthaginian dome; in modern times, after Romanesque architecture comes the Gothic. And if we separate each of these three divisions, we shall find that the three elder sisters, Hindu, Egyptian, and Roman architecture, stand for the same idea,—namely, theocracy, caste, unity, dogma, God,—and that the three younger sisters, Phenician, Greek, Gothic, whatever the diversity of expression inherent in their nature, have also the same significance,—liberty, the people, humanity.

Call him Brahmin, Magi, or Pope, according as you speak of Hindu, Egyptian, or Roman buildings, it is always the priest, and nothing but the priest. Very different are the architectures of the people: they are more opulent and less saintly. In the Phenician you see the merchant, in the Greek the republican, in the Gothic the burgess.

The general characteristics of all theocratic architectures are immutability, horror of progress, strict adherence to traditional lines, the consecration of primitive types, the adaptation of every aspect of man and nature to the incomprehensible whims of symbolism. Dark and mysterious book, which only the initiated can decipher! Furthermore, every form, every deformity even, in them has a meaning which renders it inviolable.

On the other hand, the main characteristics of the popular architectures are diversity, progress, originality, richness of design, perpetual change. They are already sufficiently detached from religion to take thought for their beauty, to tend it, to alter and improve without ceasing their garniture of statues and arabesques. They go with their times. They have something human in them which they continue to express themselves. Here you get edifices accessible to every spirit, every intelligence, every imagination; symbolic still, but as easily understood as the signs of Nature. Between this style of architecture and the theocratic there is the same difference as between the sacred and the vulgar tongue, between hieroglyphics and art, between Solomon and Phidias.

In fact, if we sum up what we have just roughly pointed out, disregarding a thousand details of proof and also exceptions to the rule, it comes briefly to this: that down to the 15th century architecture was the chief recorder of the human race; that during that space no single thought that went beyond the absolutely fundamental but was embodied in some edifice; that every popular idea, like every religious law, has had its monuments; finally, that the human race has never conceived an important thought that it has not written down in stone. And why? Because every thought, whether religious or philosophic, is anxious to be perpetuated; because the idea that has stirred one generation longs to stir others, and to leave some lasting trace.

But how precarious is the immortality of the manuscript! How far more solid, enduring, and resisting a book is the edifice! To destroy the written word there is need only of a torch and a Turk. To destroy the constructed word there is need of a social revolution, a terrestrial upheaval. The barbarians swept over the Coliseum; the deluge, perhaps, over the Pyramids.

In the 15th century all is changed. Human thought discovers a means of perpetuating itself, not only more durable and more resisting than architecture, but also simpler and more easy of achievement. Architecture is dethroned, the stone letters of Orpheus must give way to Gutenberg's letters of lead.

The Beginning of Masonry

The writer is a firm believer in the extreme antiquity of the speculative philosophy now known to the world as Freemasonry. He credits it with a continuous and unbroken existence extending in one form or another over a period of at least 6,000 years. All the groundwork connecting the mid-period history of Freemasonry with the Dionysiac artificers, the *Collegia Romana*, the Comacine architects, the medieval temple and cathedral builders, etc., may be conceded without argument and is probably correct —but none of it goes far enough. Only sentimental reasons have ever been given for these associations of mystic architects and builders, while most writers take it blandly for granted that the average mortar mixer of ancient days was a learned mystic as well. Friendship, morality, and brotherly love have doubtless played great and inspiring parts in cementing such numbers of brethren of the rule and plumb; but they have been the consequences, not the incentives, of such unions. These noble attributes ruled *in* but not *over* them.

Freemasonry has to a certain extent shared the fate and followed the course of all organizations of like weight and character, in completely surviving all recollection of its primal impulse; but we must consider that its founders were dealing with a system of perpetuating truth by means of imperishable symbols, and that they must have originally foreseen that this system would survive without the aid of either written record or graphic key to its mysteries. If we are able to justify this by proving that such a system might be started at this or any other age of the world, we shall make no incredible statement in averring that such was the beginning of our ancient craft. Every phrase of our ritual is fraught with such meaning, every obligation is couched in phraseology that admits of no other construction.

Freemasonry possesses the most stupendous and awe-inspiring secret ever imparted by revelation of Deity to mankind. It is not, however, an unknowable or unknown secret. It is the precious heritage of Freemasonry's greatest existing antagonist, the Church of Rome, of the Sufi of Mohammedanism, the Druse of Syria, the Parsees and Brahmins of India and the Lamas of

11

Tibet. It was the mystery of the ancient Magi, of the founders of the faiths of Babylonia and Assyria, of Egypt and Phenicia, of Greece and Rome, of the Druids of Gaul, the Mithraics of Persia, the patriarchs of the Jews, and the sponsors of Christianity. Only the modern Masonry of the western world ignores it, intoning over and over again the subtle keywords that should serve to unlock the hidden treasure to every initiate, passing incessantly in review the symbolic secrets that exacted the homage of the builders of the Pyramids and were still known to a select few among the founders of the modern craft in the 18th century, without knowing the occult sense of that which it idly repeats.

No oath nor obligation today hedges about the onetime deepest wisdom that man was able to attain,—a wisdom that even the lapse of ages and majestic strides of modern science have failed to render obsolete; for it is all science in one, the law of harmony that rules the universe. This was the science of "thrice-great" Hermes, of Zoroaster, Moses, Buddha, Pythagoras, and Jesus, proclaimed by each to those who could understand the language in which it was permitted them to reveal and which may, even now, be interpreted to the worthy and well qualified.

If this secret have any message for our time and conditions greater than it has ever borne to humanity, it is the much-needed lesson of the end of all controversy in the Brotherhood of Man under the Fatherhood of God. It is more than a sentiment, more than a chance or a coincidence, this wedding of a pure religious contemplation of an only true and living God to the materials, tools, and implements of architecture, this undeviating adherence to the ritualism of a mishandled race, which of all peoples of the earth, has preserved and handed down the notion of Deity as a Shepherd of Lambs and a Divine Patron of Architecture addressing his holy prophets in the language, sometimes of one and sometimes of the other.

It is in the age-long absence of anything like systematic pursuit of the clues arising from these facts that Freemasonry has become a sort of intellectual no-man's land, open to the assaults of the wildest conjecture and most trivial speculation.

On this latter basis, almost exclusively, has the literature of the craft been built up. It is only within the last few years that have appeared a few well-considered studies of the more salient phases which have not been intended to prop up some improbable theory. The mathematical, geometrical, architectural, astronomical, and other pointed allusions of our ritual have been well recognized and ably commented upon; but most of them are biblical in origin, and it has not seemed to occur to the commentators that a day was approaching when our Great Light, as well, would reveal still greater truths than were perceived by our forefathers, from literal interpretation of cabalistic texts destroyed by translation into foreign tongues.

It is therefore obvious that there can be no successful Masonic research that is not also biblical research, reverently and patiently conducted, for the purpose of ascertaining the precise connecting links that have raised up, in addition to innumerable religious bodies, an auxiliary organization counting its votaries by the million which, while disavowing sectarianism, is nevertheless one of the most militant, persistent, and potent factors for the uplift of humanity and the perpetuation of divine worship that the world has ever known.

Theosophy and Masonry

There is an extensive volume of literature based on the assumption by Theosophists that Theosophists are the old original Freemasons, and that their esoteric teachings contain all that is of value in Freemasonry and reach far beyond it. It will suffice merely to quote Dr. J. E. Buck's "Mystic Masonry," Rev. C. H. Vail's "Ancient Mysteries and Modern Masonry," and "The Great Work" by T. K. to supply most entertaining examples of this interesting idea. All of these are painstaking and certainly scholarly attempts to assert a connection between Theosophy and Freemasonry. There are several student bodies of Masonic Theosophists, or Theosophical Masons—whichever sounds more acceptable. Several of the best known and most capable Masonic essayists in this country and in England are ardent Theosophists, whose voluminous writings are always full of allusions to Masonry as a collateral branch of their favorite speculation.

We wish to be entirely respectful to both those who do and those who do not credit a connection between Masonry and Theosophy.

Taking the entire ritual of the three degrees of the Blue Lodge, as we know them, and in addition the Mark Master and Royal Arch degrees, no such things as constitute what avowed Theosophists call "Theosophy" are taught in them. The moment, however, that the analytical mind begins to dwell upon the intricacies of the Masonic ritual and its spirited action in dramatic presentation, it is perceived that every phrase is a studied allusion to something far deeper than the proffered explanation. This profundity is not an illusion. It is thoroughly genuine; but it is not specifically accounted for in any part of our work beyond the intimation that diligent search will be rewarded with ultimate truth if the seeker persevere to the end. One may speak more plainly of ''Theosophy,'' meaning simply ''God-Wisdom'' or ''God's Truth,'' which is secret only in so far as the uninstructed are unable to comprehend its abstruse phraseology, the key words of which are largely from the Sanskrit.

The moment that Theosophy becomes dogmatic it departs from the original intention of its modern sponsors and becomes at least a religion in the making. We cannot concern ourselves with the immortal characters or perpetual reincarnation of ''Masters,'' or in the vague stories of secret hoards of wisdom buried in caves among the Himalayas, and the catalepsies and clairvoyances of ''adepts,'' because, unless we be ''adepts'' ourselves, in which case we should have no need to ask questions, we have no means of discriminating among the genuine, the self-deluded, and the impostor,—the inevitable trinity of all so-called ''occult'' investigation.

The term ''Theosophy'' is so elastic that it can be made to embrace every species of speculation in matters guarded under a veil of secrecy, and such is certainly the case so far as most American Theosophists are concerned. The fact that Masonry is ancient, guarded, and in a sense scientific sets up a series of analogies with that which Theosophy claims, rendering it extremely easy for an enthusiast, versed in both systems, to establish a series of parallels of great plausibility. It is only borrowing one of the favorite reasonings of the Theosophists themselves to express an opinion that both are descended by different channels from an identical source.

The Ancient Mysteries

''The Ancient Mysteries'' is a modern term invented for the purpose of gathering under a single specific classification all the curious rites, ceremonies, and ritualistic allusions of prechristian ages which are described to us in classic works. None of these documents enlighten us upon other than the externals. They tell us far less of what transpired in the ancient Temples of Initiation than the curious bystander may learn of modern Masonry by mere dint of keeping his ears open.

While analogies without end are discernible between our

own secret work and some of the traditions of ancient initiations, what has been held back for the advancement of science during our present age to reveal, has been the fundamental philosophy of which these ceremonies were merely illustrative.

Up to a few years ago, the dramatic action of the Ancient Mysteries was, so far as any one was able to give a reasonable explanation of it, completely devoid of sense; but the penetration of European savants into the wealth of Oriental sacred and philosophical literature has unlocked a mine of precise information heretofore unimaginable.

No matter who or what constituted the prehistoric population of ancient Europe and Asia Minor, the fact is that it was always inferior to and doomed to disappear or be absorbed by the great Indo-Germanic invasions, which swarmed westward, at intervals, from a central home, somewhere at the foot of the Hindu-Kush Mountains. Extensive invasions of both white and yellow Asiatics were successive and continuous, over many hundred years. The last on record was that of the Huns under Attila, if we except the Turks.

They must have begun, however, at least 5,000 to 7,000 years before the Christian era. It was when this Aryan people was still locked in the bosom of central Asia that the mind of man first began to speculate in the higher mathematics and the beginning of science began to supplant mere childish wonder and barbarous fetishism. Mathematics and geometry, joined to an ardent pursuit of astronomy in regions most favorable to observation where only the naked eye was to be depended on, were made the basis of all human speculation upon the nature and attributes of the Infinite. It must be remembered that it was only well within the Christian era that every human consideration was supposed to be so dependent upon planetary influences that the entire science of medicine consisted in the selection of plant, animal, and mineral substances, which because of their planetary affinities would counteract human ills.

For thousands of years nothing could be begun, pursued, or finished without consulting the stars for propitious occasions, and so a vast system of philosophy was gradually built up of those three scientific ingredients.

The Secret Doctrine

This original philosophy is really the foundation of what Theosophists call the "Secret Doctrine," and the initiatory ceremonies by which men were inducted into its enlightening presence were what we now call the ''Ancient Mysteries,'' many of the symbols of which still survive in the Masonic Lodge.

The advancement of understanding in these ''Secret Doctrines'' received a setback through hundreds of years on the part of organizations that wished to monopolize all knowledge and practice of the Ancient Mysteries, and it has been only during the last century that the great gulfs that separated Occident and Orient have been successfully bridged by savants who have, piece by piece, reconstructed the whole ancient fabric.

Egypt, Assyria, Babylonia, Persia, and India are every day yielding up long buried secrets, which throw a bright noonday glare upon the real derivations and significances of hitherto cabalistic dogmas; which are not proved untrue, but truer in altered senses than were ever dreamed of. Under the protection of modern toleration, work is being done by excavators on the sites of ancient cities and translators of long buried documentary testimony to the participation of our ancient brethren in all of our most interesting philosophical speculations and how close they approached us in actual mental achievement. The persecution of one Galileo or the holocaust of 100,000 Huguenots would today be insufficient to stem the tide of discovery.

Theosophy is based upon a study of the ''Secret Doctrine'' derived by modern students from Indian (Hindu) sources direct. Masonry is what is left, after centuries of vicissitude, of its western development. In neither case was the original fund one of deception or charlatanism; but, let us again repeat, it was ''the science of the ancient world'' expressed. through reverence, in terms of awe-fraught mysticism.

The Hermetic Philosophy

The so-called ''Hermetic Philosophy'' is much quoted by the older writers on the subject of Masonry, and one encounters references to it in the works of the greatest of them all, the venerable Albert Pike. Bro. Pike says of the reputed founder of the so-called Hermetic School:

''From the bosom of Egypt sprang a man of consummate wisdom, initiated in the secret knowledge of India, of Persia, and of Ethiopia, named Thoth or Phtha by his compatriots, Taaut by the Phenicians and *Hermes Trismegistus* (Thrice Great Hermes) by the Greeks. In Egypt he instituted hieroglyphics; he selected a certain number of persons, whom he judged fitted to be the depositaries of his secrets, of only such as were capable of attaining the throne and the first offices in the mysteries, he united them in a body, created them *priests of the living God*, instructed them in the sciences and arts, especially astronomy, music (which he is said to have *invented*), arithmetic, and work in metals, etc. Under him, Egypt paid homage to *seven* principal deities'' (the seven planets).

This is condensing into very small compass a great mass of material which has come down to us about a legendary mortal, whose every attribute as recorded is little short of miraculous, and whose supposed writings, Bro. Pike shows us, greatly influenced the early Christian fathers, particularly Saint Augustine, who held them in great reverence.

HERMIS TRISMEGISTUS.
Note the Scorpion, sign of his station in the "South." The Ibis hieroglyphic shows his identity with Thoth.

The name ''Hermetic'' has become synonymous with ''concealment'' or ''mysterious.'' Our naive forefathers certainly gave little trouble to the mystery mongers; but seemed to exercise their powers of credence like a professional strong man his muscles. They saw little to wonder at in the million and one familiar things that are the marvels of science today; but seemingly laid great value upon a capacity for asserting the impossible. It was the ''long suit'' of the wise man of once-upon-a-time to affirm ''two and two make six, and to prove it I will change this stick into a serpent.''

There is no doubt, however, that the ''Hermetic Wisdom'' merits every eulogy that could possibly be bestowed upon it; for it was the collective science of the ancient world, so called because attributed by the Magian astronomers—or rather Astrologers; for the stars were studied for omens, not physical facts—to the influence of the planet Mercury.

The name ''Mercury,'' or *Mercurius*, was the Latin translation of the Greek *Hermes*. Like almost all astronomical names of both Greece and Rome, it is a corruption of the Syrian *Mar Kurios* (''Son of the Lord''—Sun), which in turn is a literal translation of *ChR-Mes* (Horus-Moses, ''the Son of Horus''). The custom of referring all inspirational writings to their spiritual source was the cause of the attribution to the celestial Hermes of a stupendous volume of ancient literature. He is called "the Author of 20,000 volumes," just as to Nebo—precisely the same planet Mercury as known 2,000 years before to the Babylonians—were attributed all the sacred writings of their priests.

The British Museum catalogue of Babylonian and Assyrian antiquities states that "Almost every tablet of importance in the Royal Library of Nineveh," most of which have been recovered by the Museum through Prof. Layard and others, "bears upon it the following words: 'The palace of Ashur-Ban-i-Pal, King of Hosts, King of Assyria, who putteth his trust in the gods Ashur and Belit, on whom Nabu and Tashmetu have bestowed ears which hear and eyes which see. I have inscribed upon tablets the noble products of the work of the scribe, which none of the Kings who have gone before me had learned, together with *the Wisdom* of *Nabu* (Nebo-Hermes) so far as it existeth.' "

As Ashur-Ban-i-Pal reigned in the seventh century B. C., this is a pretty respectable date for Hermetic writings already. Among the tablets enumerated is found the world famous "Creation Tablet."

We quote the following from Rev. Joseph Fort Newton's book, "The Builders": "The cube was a sacred emblem of the Lydian Kubele, known to the Romans in after ages as Ceres or Cybele; hence, as some aver, the derivation of the word 'Cube.' Mercury, Apollo, Neptune, and Hercules were worshiped under the form of a square stone; while a large black stone was the emblem of Buddha among the Hindoos, of Manah Theus-Ceres in Arabia, and of Odin in Scandinavia."

Nebo in ancient Babylonia and Assyria, Thoth (later Serapis) in Egypt, Taaut in Phenicia, Daud in Palestine, Apollo, Hermes, Mercury, among the Greeks and Romans, Odin in Scandinavia, and Buddha in India are *all one and the same planet Mercury,* the planet nearest to and inseparable companion to the Sun, part of the year rising heliacally—that is to say, seen for a few moments at dawn until obscured by the sun's greater light, when it was called "Apollo"—and at another season, at evening, as the Sun's light grows dim, when it was called "Mercury" ("Messenger of the Gods").

Symbols of the Hermetic Philosophy: Sulphur—Mercury—Salt.

Now, in the astrological arrangement by the ancient Chaldeans of the planets in the Mansions or Houses of the Zodiac the Moon and the Sun are placed side by side in Cancer and Leo, respectively. The "Night" house of Mercury* is in Gemini at the *left* of Cancer, and his "day" house is in Virgo, to the right of Leo. Therefore the center of the zodiacal east is marked by a Triad of Sun, Moon and Mercury; which those read in Alchemistic and Rosicrucian lore will not fail to recognize as the central postulate of both of those famous philosophies. They were the lesser lights of earlier rituals.

Virgo is Demeter or Ceres, and consequently the Kubele and Cybele of the "square stone"; Gemini, the twins, are the youthful Hercules and Apollo ("Strength and Beauty"); while Hermes, in the house of Demeter (Virgo), is the Divine Wisdom—for it must be remembered that to the initiate all these pagan deities were but the attributes, emanations, or perceptible qualities of the "One" God, no matter what the "profane" imagined them to be.

As the secret wisdom of the alchemists, developed from the ancient Hebrew *Kabbalah,* tells us, the combination of "sulphur, salt and mercury" is that which produces the "living Gold," mercury being denoted the "bond" that unites the other two. The alchemical signs for these three elements—or rather four, for under the first, sulphur, was hidden "fire," under the second, "earth," and under (two signs of) Mercury, air and water"— were respectively the sun, moon and the planet Mercury. Alchemy was really a secret school of philosophy, teaching the same truths as Masonry once taught, only employing the terminology of the chemist and refiner of metals instead of that of the builder.

By this combination is really meant the threefold nature of man—the "soul," which the ancients held to emanate from the sun; the "body," which came under the special influence of the moon; and "spirit," or mental intelligence, which was the gift of Hermes or Mercury—the "mind," or *manas,* as it was called in Sanskrit, being that which specifically constituted "man."

There is every reason to believe that this doctrine underlay the entire fabric of ancient philosophical paganism, and that the reason why it has not descended to us in the classics is just because it was the "Hermetic" or sealed wisdom. Pillars were anciently dedicated to Hermes, and the secret of the "ashlars" is closely connected with the double personality of this same old divinity. Hermes became, in the course of many transforma-

*See Page 100

tions, the archangel Raphael, and has always been the peculiar tutelary genius of "man."

The historical Buddha (Gautama Sakyamouni) must not be confounded with the Aryan *Buddhi* (the Divine Wisdom), still the name of the planet Mercury in India. From India, where it was once Bo-den, the Indo-Germanic races carried this divinity, as Wo-den or Odin, to the farthest confines of Scandinavia. The day of Mercury has always been what is the present Buddhist "sabbath." Wednesday.

Rosicrucianism and Freemasonry

We frequently hear of an alleged connection between Freemasonry and so-called "Rosicrucianism" brotherhoods. In the course of the last couple of centuries there have been many hundred claims set up to the title of "Society" or "Fraternity" of the Rosy Cross. Any brother who feels inclined to dip into the question of extinct Masonic rites and degrees, by a short course of Mackey's Masonic Encyclopedia, will be, if not already informed, astonished to find that all the Masonry we are officially aware of today is but a mere fragment of all that has at one time or other figured as of impressive importance to the craft.

In the archives of the Scottish Rite are preserved evidences of the voluntary abdications of a number of imposing Masonic "rites" that once enjoyed high favor and numerous membership, but which eventually dissolved, under pressure of internal dissensions, and the larger hope embodied in the rise of a body so constituted as to obviate the possibility of unbecoming strife and other weaknesses.

At the present moment the empty dignities and now meaningless powers of obsolete rites are occasionally heard of as passed from hand to hand, for trifling money considerations, wherever a gull can be induced to believe that he is receiving high Masonic degrees, even though the same may be conferred upon him by a single individual "by virtue of powers," etc., in a basement dining room or hall bedroom.

The chief significance that attaches itself to the revival of interest in the Rosicrucians lies in the fact that, according to the strict spirit of the ancient brotherhood, there can be but *one* organization in existence entitled to their name and secrets, and that organization never had nor, it is claimed, never will have any public or exoteric existence. It is not the sort of club or society that has officers, holds public or even private meetings and elects eligible persons to membership.

The true Rosicrucian may never meet another of his mystic order on the physical plane. He is not initiated in a hall or chapter room after having paid a fee; but it is made known to him by occult means that he has been found worthy of admission into this literal band of immortals, and thereafter he is shown how to project his perceptions on to a higher plane upon which it is possible for him to meet, know and commune with all his fellow members, who assemble like witches upon a *sabbat,* in a twinkling of an eye, by merely willing to do so, no matter where their physical bodies may happen to be sojourning.

In fact, the first public gossip concerning the Rosicrucians and their wonderful powers began to be bruited about at the beginning of the seventeenth century. Membership in the fraternity was attributed to various alchemists by the herd, and claimed by numerous charlatans on the other hand. Many tales are told of the discovery of weird underground vaults in otherwise desert places, which upon being opened were found to be brilliantly illuminated by perpetually burning lamps—that is to say, until extinguished by the admission of outer air. These were said to have been the secret meeting places of the Rosicrucians.

From the very nature of Rosicrucianism as described, however, that of tradition must necessarily be spurious, as the mere fact of publicity, upon however private or restricted a scale, is sufficient to stamp it as such. The existence of Rosicrucianism might be claimed, and certain highly endowed scholars and scientists be suspected—nay, openly charged—with being members of its charmed circle; but no genuine record exists of any ancient Rosicrucian Society upon which any theory of continuity might be based by a modern group of students of the occult.

There is quite a successful modern Rosicrucian Society in London, the moving spirit of which was the late Dr. Wynn Westcott, formerly coroner for the County of Middlesex. As a research body, disinterring many interesting legends about the reputed Rosicrucians of the Middle Ages, this latter day society has done good work.

It all sums up in the state of mind of the person most interested. An old Potsdam pensioner once wrote King Frederick the Great in much distress over the suppression of a military decoration, the only one he had ever received. The king smilingly wrote on the margin of the complaint, "Pensioner X has herewith our royal permission to wear all the abolished decorations he likes."

Just as the evolutionary process, through which all organic

beings have arrived from lower forms to present high states of development, may be traced in the structures of those beings themselves, so the structure of any mystical order claiming extraordinary antiquity will reveal the foundation of its claims to the student, irrespective of any personal contentions.

Our own craft has hardly departed from the use of ancient monitors and lectures connecting Masonry with the beginnings of the human race—Adam, Seth, Enoch, Noah, Moses, and other patriarchs—which had become a laughing stock among our strenuous modernists, when it begins to transpire that the structure of Freemasonry is superior to her traditions, and that he who knows Masonry structurally will have no difficulty whatever in comprehending all these curious connections as apt and purposeful.

When this knowledge becomes more common to the fraternity we shall be in a position to understand the difference between that which guarantees the genuineness of our own antiquity and the claims that any mystical brotherhood may at present set up, of surpassing age, royal descent, and the possession of the fundamental *arcane* of the universe, without the average Mason's being able to prove that his pretensions have any greater value than those of the newcomer.

God and Masonry

There is no place in Masonry for dogmatic controversy affecting the current convictions of brethren of the craft. In its highest contemplation Freemasonry solely regards and addresses itself to the "Great Architect of the Universe," respecting the Names under which this Unique Identity is apostrophized in every clime, by every race, and by every school of thought.

There are no religious differences attached to the adoration of the Supreme Being. Men differ alone with respect to some of His manifestations of love and solicitude for humanity, making claims to an exclusiveness in one respect or another, which are too often the outgrowth of fast-vanishing racial isolations and the diverse trends of thought consequent upon differences of origin, climate, and environment.

In quibbling over these differences, so frequently the result of misunderstandings of identical premises, viewed from diverging angles, men are too prone to forget that the goodness and providence of Almighty God is forever pouring in a mighty deluge upon us, manifesting itself unceasingly and impartially in everything that either experiences or can be experienced. From the selfish standpoint of the unintelligent ego, each individual is alternately blessed with satisfactions and cursed with deprivations or distresses, the extremes predominating in many instances without apparent reason. Many of the ancient philosophers, therefore, taught that man could attain supreme contentment only by realizing his identity with the All. Sensing this, he perceived the resistless operation of the great laws of Being, in perfect poise, harmony, and impartiality, requiring only to be heeded for man to escape the evils and enjoy the benefits thereof during his allotted term, the accidents and mishaps befalling him not being subject to the caprices of an unpropitious Ruler, but consequent upon his own unguarded collisions with unchangeable law.

Therefore the whole problem of human life became the attainment of greater and ever greater knowledge of the natural law, upon which all progress and all security to life and happiness depended in so eminent a degree, and the divine gift of the reasoning faculties, which rendered this possible, was appreciated as God's most precious blessing to man. Thousands of years of experiment and ceaseless vigilance on the part of eager watchers have never resulted in the detection of a single principle so unrelated to the rest of the universal machine as to have no dependence upon it. Even where the wonders of science have disclosed marvels so intricate as to baffle explanation or analysis, they have at least proved so entirely subject to certain conditions of known factors as to be easily provoked into manifestation or suppressed from view, at the will of man.

Year by year, day by day, hour by hour, minute by minute, the infinite details of this great cosmos-pervading law keep on unfolding to human perception, filling all space with their greatness and mocking pursuit in their ultramicroscopic perfections and yet nothing is discovered that had not existence ages before the human mind began to concern itself with its intricacies. The capacity of mind to see and understand has limitations, and history—that of which it takes cognizance through the medium of the senses—is limitless and without historical beginning or end.

Every past age has attempted to place bounds upon that which it is legitimate for man to know or think he knows about the origin and constitution of the wonders about him. Each era has closed its book of human knowledge with a flaming "Finis" at the end of an ultimate chapter, and yet the dawn of every other day has ushered in new wonders, new visions, and new truths.

"Dogma" is the name given to all these futile finalities which do not finish, to the barbed wire entanglements and *chevaux de frise* set by each generation at the limit of its attainments, in the vain thought that the "End" had been achieved.

In most cases dogmas will be found to revolve round the privilege of classes to rule masses, irrespective of the fact that part of the cosmic law is as sure and continual an oxygenation of the sea of humanity by waves of upheaval as is manifest in seas of water, in which that which is the sluggish depth of today may be the foam-crested wave of tomorrow. Yet the mind of man, framed in the image of the Creator, even as the receiver of an acoustic instrument must be attuned to the vibrations of the transmittor, that the message may be received as it is sent, has discovered constant and unchanging elements in this stupendous order of varied manifestations, has discovered chaos-banishing laws which must be the same in an atom as in a sun, and so may be exhibited in symbols of dimensions convenient to the stature of contemplative man.

Such are the symbols of Freemasonry—evidences of the truth attributed to Triple-great Hermes, the mystic founder of our craft, that "that which is above may be discovered by examination of that which is below."

The Masonic student may concern himself with every branch of research that is capable of throwing light upon the causes that have led men to crystallize their perceptions of immutable law in emblems and symbols. He may pursue each of the various paths of investigation indicated by the obscure phraseology of ritual until he emerges into the full blaze of Masonic light embracing its fundamental truth. He may unravel the intricacies of ancient philosophies and mythologies, in order to convince himself of their ultimate source in the fountain of revealed wisdom, and he may set his own value upon anthropomorphisms or the embodiment of attributes and principles in fleshly guise, so that what really are the play of natural forces, the sport of the elements, the cycles of worlds, are described in terms taken from the vocabulary of human life. Yet, with all this, he may not consciously offend his brother, by striking at the latter's highest individual spiritual contemplations in a humor of disdain or ridicule. Each mind is a universe in little, a cell of the universe in great, one as eternal as the other, and subject to the same law of gradual unfoldment. Some day we shall all know the intricate and the complicated as we at present know that which is simple and few of parts; but of the infinite aggregate, the unfathomable indivisible total, our Masonry teaches us the value. NOW.

Masonry's Real Secret

Freemasonry is not only all that its most enthusiastic panegyrist ever proclaimed it to be on sentimental, moral, and fraternal grounds, but it is fundamentally and structurally a system of natural theology, *proving* the existence and attributes of the one true God to the satisfaction of the intellect, and so supplying a bulwark to faith unattainable by any other means. The nature of this proof, although formulated before the pyramids were built, is not so abstruse as might at first be imagined, and is founded on precisely the same assumption as the natural theology of a Paley or a Brougham of our own era—that *evidence of design or intention proves the presence of Mind,* the wisdom, power, and beauty of which may be inferred from the result.

As in natural theology we look for evidence of a thinking, contriving, planning, improving, wise and beneficent Mind of infinite volume, controlling and directing all things, so let us search among the remaining relics of our remote ancestors for evidence, that, as Kipling exquisitely sings in his ballad of the "Builder," "They too had known." The evidence is incontrovertible, and Masonry is the evidence.

Ancient priesthood believed that the great mass of mankind was too undeveloped to comprehend a philosophy of divinity based upon more or less scientific premises. Therefore, they carefully conserved their special knowledge, imparting it only to chosen initiates, while treating the masses to a spectacular exoteric system. Such was in fact the origin of the dual system that has prevailed through the ages, which was as much a part of Judaism and primitive and mediaeval Christianity as of the pagan idolatries, by which the priests *knew* and the people *thought they knew.*

Even some of our most common superstitions are relics of this state of things. All the prejudice popularly entertained against the number 13 resides not in its "unluckiness," but because it was the key to religious mysteries that the priests did not wish the people to penetrate; hence, if a man started to run every time he encountered this number and would refuse to think of it for fear of breaking his leg, the sacerdotal interests were safe.

When the period approached that the average citizen knew more than the hierophant of former years, he was not encouraged, but repressed, and instead of being admitted to the Mysteries was driven back with curses, so that the priestly caste might retain its ascendancy. Notable exceptions to this were the examples of Egypt and Greece, where enlightenment was, at certain ages, almost universal. It was the suppression of the Mysteries that enslaved Europe for centuries.

If the ultimate and all-sustaining secret of Freemasonry may be openly expressed in a few words, it will be these:

The entire course of nature is manifested in cycles. Some of these are scientifically real, others are but appearances based upon the presence and position of the observer upon the earth, away from which they have no true existence. For instance, there is no night except as we are temporarily on the shadow side of our globe during its diurnal rotation. There is this movement of the earth upon its axis; there is the annual revolution that we term the year; and there is the stupendous cycle called the precession of the equinoxes, which requires nearly 26,000 years for its accomplishment.

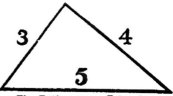

The Pythagorean Triangle.

There are the relative velocities and courses of the planets, the axial revolution of the sun, their angles of inclination, the atomic weights of metals, the phenomena of light, color, crystalization, and gravitation. These can be technically expressed in no other way than in terms of mathematics and geometry. When the results are expressed in their simplest forms, the latter prove to be the same rudimentary geometrical figures that supply the structure of crystals, and all blend together into the marvelous triangle that caused old Pythagoras to cry "Eureka!" when its beauties burst upon him.

By careful computation we are able to reconstruct this really divine system, and we find that the exact proportions relating to the celestial correlations in question were lavishly and exclusively employed in the architecture of all the temples of old, in all the culture lands of the world, both east and west. Still greater does our wonder grow when we recognize in lodge and chapter the whole mechanism of this wonderful natural science, and what was before hidden and dark bursts upon us as a beautiful, perfect, and complete whole.

Pythagoras and Freemasonry

The man whose name will always be indelibly associated with the above Triangle and the celebrated figure called the "47th Problem of Euclid" derived from it, is the great Greek Initiate and Teacher, Pythagoras of Krotona (B. C. 570-500).

We frequently see it called into question as to whether Pythagoras and his famous problem had really anything to do with the foundation of Freemasonry as the older writers on the subject claim. Personally he wrote nothing.

His principal chroniclers were Philolaus (B. C. 370) and Jamblichus (A. D. 340). He is quoted and otherwise referred to by many others, and what we learn of his philosophy from these sources indicates that the "number philosophy" of the Gnostic sect of Marcionites strongly resembled it. A great revival of Pythagorean philosophy took place in Europe during the latter part of the 17th century, just at the period when Freemasonry began to attract public attention.

Johannes Meursius (1620), Marcus Meibonius (1650), and Athanasius Kircher (a Jesuit, 1660) collected and republished all the fragments they could find from the preceding authorities.

If Pythagoras studied philosophy among the Medean Magi at Babylon—and the records at least state that he was a pupil of the Chaldeans—he imbibed from them the pure Semitic philosophy thus expressed in his transmitted sayings:

"The Monad is God and the good, which is the origin of the *One* and is itself Intelligence. The Monad is the beginning of everything. Unity is the principle of all things."

If Pythagoras was, as credibly stated, initiated into the Eleusinian Mysteries in Greece, the Mysteries of Isis in Egypt, and the Brahmanic Mysteries at Elephanta and Ellora, India, he learned the same truth in each of these places, where the *Apporheta* communicated to the *Epopt* (i. e., supreme secret disclosed to the highest initiate) was always the same, viz., that there is but ONE God. The great crime of the ancient world was that it reserved this fact to initiates alone and publicly taught a pantheism,

27

which to Adepts was a veiled philosophy, while the masses viewed it as a multiplicity of independent gods and goddesses.

We have archeological remains of the highest antiquity to prove that this problem of the right-angled triangle of 3-4-5, of which the Euclidian figure is *but one of several possible extensions,* was the central symbol of the religion of widely dispersed millions during many centuries.

The theorems of the sacred geometry of the ancient philosophers are *not included in the works of Euclid,* even though subject to the same mechanical laws he expounds. This "sacred geometry," which is the branch underlying all Masonic symbolism, was not intended for the purpose of teaching Operative Masons how to make truly square corners, but for the far more noble and glorious purpose of demonstrating the unity of God, the likeness of the human mind to the divine mind, the omnipotence and omnipresence of God, and the immortality of the soul.

Waving aside the fact that 3 is a *male* number because odd, and 4 *female* because even (3 representing Osiris, 4 Isis, and 5 Horus), the importance of "the triangle of Huramon" (*Horus-Ammon-Hiram*), ages older than Pythagoras, as a human contemplation and coequal with creation as a divine principle, resides in the fact that it was the center, core, or nucleus of the ancient sacred philosophy, to which we owe so much. Its symbol for at least 5,000 years has been an eye, now the "all-seeing

"The Eye of Horus."

eye" of Freemasonry. From it emanated, as a plant from a seed, the various canons of symmetry and order (time, space, number, and proportion), which still reign over the heart and intelligence of man, for man does not regard as beautiful that which his eyes show him by consensus of agreement to be ugly. His recognition of the fitness of certain forms and the laws of their combinations is as much a part of nature as gravity and electricity.

Quite as true as the fact that the perception of the wonderful truths we have enumerated was just cause for Brother Pythagoras to have indulged in the somewhat extravagant barbecue attributed to him, is the circumstance that the prehistoric Mound Builders of America employed this same Pythagorean triangle to demonstrate the fourth dimension.

The "Forty-Seventh Problem"

The so-called "forty-seventh problem of Euclid" was undoubtedly regarded by the ancient mystics as a divinely appointed

Canon of Universal harmony, to the fundamental mathematical truth of which might be traced most of the laws of symmetry and order, which reign throughout the vast expanse of Cosmos. The precise nature of the various connections must be established by analogies, rather than by concrete examples, because the peculiar geometrical figure, in question, was probably deemed one of the sacred mysteries by the ancients and peculiarly one which might not be hewn, cut, carved or marked in any manner by which it might become legible or intelligible to the profane.

Clay Tessera found in an Egyptian Tomb.

Its delineation, graphically, we probably first owe to the Arab geometers of the early days of our present era, among whom no scruple could have prevailed. The only truly ancient example the writer has ever seen is on a little clay *Tessera* from an Egyptian tomb forty centuries old, upon which it is rudely, but unmistakably, present.

The psychology of geometrical science to the sympathetic student is as thrilling as that of music or color to specialists therein.

There are marvels in Mathematics, indeed, but in Geometry, mathematics are applied and every point, line, superficies and solid, in its relations and potentialities bespeaks a subtle something which Finite Mind instinctively recognizes as the production of Infinite Mind.

We would be utterly unable to realize, much less formulate the notion of "Law," pervading Cosmos, if all facts and forces did not present unswerving, uncompromising obedience to the geometrical verities which are at the root of all of that which we term "Manifestation"—visualized existence.

Of the limited volume of these fundamental geometrical laws—and there are surprisingly few to account for the splendors of the Universe they present to our vision, the fact that the *hypothenuse* of a right-angle of three to four, invariably and to the ultra-microscopic fraction, measures five, as we have seen, is one of the most perfect proofs of pre-determined plan. The resulting triangle of 3-4-5 is not the only example of such a correlation between exact quantities, for Geometry is full of them, but it is the simplest and most basic and calls attention to countless other remarkable factors to the cosmic whole, to which its intimate relationship may be demonstrated.

It would naturally be a physical impossibility to cover the

enormous ground available for discussion, within present limits, but some slight notion of the tremendous influence of Geometry in general and this notable Pythagorean proposition, in particular, upon the philosophies and theologies of the World, may be obtained by deciphering a few ancient occultisms concerning it.

In order to get our bearing, we are compelled to formulate an ascertained law of development in all of the latter.

Their unique basis is the recognizable and ascertainable phenomena of the Universe, the definition of which constitutes what modern man terms "Science," but which the ancient mind referred more directly to Deity, as an arbitrary power.

All such definition was necessarily confined to terms of time, space, number and proportion, which can only be expressed in those of Mathematics or Geometry, the most stupendous of all contemplations being the observation of the vast cosmic machine from an astronomical standpoint.

That which struck the ancient mind with the greatest wonder was, self evidently, the fact that if all of the wonders of the Universe resolved themselves into mathematical expressions and the latter into geometrical figures, often simple ones at that, which in turn melted into the simple fundamentals of the latter science, then in the latter must be found the dynamic concentrations which most closely approach a conception of Divinity.

A further step along the line of developing rational occultism was gained by the employment of identical characters to express both letters and numbers. That which we now call the decimal system was worked by "the power of Nine" or "three times three."

The letters of the Hebrew alphabet and the Greek letters derived from an analogous source, counted from *Aleph* or *Alpha*, 1 to *Teth* or *Theta*, 9 and from *Jod* or *Iota*, 10, to *Peh* or *Pi*, 80. Beginning with R, 200 (in Greek, 100) the Hebrew letters are one digital value higher than the corresponding Greek letters. It must also be remarked that the Hebrew letter *Vau* or 6, corresponded to the now missing *Digamma* in Greek, once placed between *Eta* and *Zeta*.

With this equipment we can now understand the significance of the ancient Hebrew Deity names, such as *Al Shdi*, Biblically translated "God Almighty," (*El Shaddai*) or $1+30+300+4+10$ —345, or 3, 4 and 5, in decimal places. Also the corresponding name *Ahih Ashr Ahih*, "I am that I am," amounting to 543, the same figures reversed, and their addition $345+543$—888, the basis of the Greek word *Jesous* or $10+8+200+70+400+200$, the true meaning of which, along a special line of demonstration, is the Solar *Logos,* or World creating, sustaining and preserving manifestations of Deity, a symbolism still dimly preserved in Masonry under the veil of a twenty-four inch gauge.

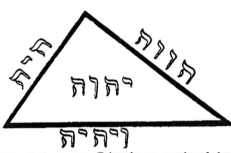

The Pythagorean Triangle as employed by the Ancient Hebrews.

The Egyptian name of *Mes,* a Son, which was that of Moses, is equal to 345, while the word "Messiah" is really *Mes Jah,* or "Son of God," a cabalism on the Pythagorean triangle, for the word *Jah* is equivalent to 16 or the sum of $3 + 4 = 7$ and $4+5=9$, the two chief cosmic numbers derived from this triangle. $3+4+5$ equalling 12, the Hebrews took the ineffable name JHVH, three times repeated and permuted the letters into HJH (3), HVVH (4), VJHJH (5), reading "He that was, He that is and He that will be" or "is to come," thus paraphrasing the declaration of Horus in the "Book of the Dead." "I am yesterday, today and tomorrow," and the inscription over the Shrine of Isis, "I Isis am all that ever has been, now is or ever will be and no mortal has ever lifted my veil."

We also know that the secret supreme being of the Egyptians was HU-HI, the Mongolian dual principle, HO and HI, which assimilated to the Sanscrit FOHAT or "Cosmic Energy" and ICHCHA, "Human Will."

It is relatively easy, now, to follow the Egyptian philosophy of the 47th problem, which attributed the square of 3 to *Asar* (Osiris), the square of 4 to *Ishah* (Isis) and the square of 5 to *Chr* (Horus). Let us remark, in passing, that *Chr* is the Sanscrit word for "Light," RCH, reversed and is the origin of the tradition that upon "discovering" the 47th problem, Pythagoras joyfully uttered the word *Eureka.* Greek mythology is full of stolen Oriental sacred words thus metamorphosed.

Asar, which is 3×54, 162, is *Ash Ra,* the Solar Fire, *Ishah* (a name still preserved in the Arabic *Ayesha*), "The Female," meaning terrestrial "Nature, 4×54 or 216, which is the sum of the cubes of 3, 4 and 5, and *Chr* the Male principle or fructifying spirit of Nature, is 2×54, or 108. All of these numbers are multiples of 9 or 3×3, and this last number, especially, is the

The "Forty-seventh Problem" was among the Ancient Egyptians the symbol of Osiris, Isis and Horus.

one defined by Hindu Astrology as the full term of human life, and thus represents humanity in the abstract. Egyptian philosophy regarded the great Cosmic process of generation and regeneration as resultant upon the infinitely reiterated passages of the Male principle through the Female principle, Father and Son being, spiritually, a Unit ("I and my Father are One").

The number 270 (9×30) represents the number, in days, of human gestation and is the sum of 162 (Father) and 108 (Son). Thus, merely supplying the natural philosophical postulate that the Father passing his vital principle through the Mother, continues to live in the Son, we secure a Pythagorean triangle of 162—216—270.

If the 47th problem be exhibited, as it frequently is, divided into alternating black and white squares. symbolic, among other things, of the "Dual principle," the division will be 26 (10+5+6 +5; JHVH) of one color and 24 (8+8+8) of the other, while the measure round-about the whole figure will be 36 spaces, giving the Pythagorean sacred number of the Sun, upon which the Sage of Samos swore his pupils to secrecy. The 9+16+25=50 squares

The "Forty-seventh Problem" a symbol of the Creative Logos.

thus gave rise to the old Greek cabalistic name of the Sun, "*Damnamenos* of the fifty faces." The Hebrews celebrated each fiftieth year as a Jubilee, calling it the "Power of the Number Twelve" (3+4+5). In present conclusion, it is regrettable that we have only just begun to enter upon the mere fringe of this wonderful subject, concerning which, if anything, may most truly be said that "the World itself could not contain all the books which might be written concerning it."*

* This paper originally appeared in   the *Acacia Journal*.

The Number-Letter System

The next step beyond that of embodying the sacred proportions in architecture and art was to contrive their vocal expression.

The ancient number-letter system of the Orient is often difficult for the Masonic student to understand; but when one looks into it carefully it is comparatively simple. In the days before the invention of symbols for figures Hebrew scholars expressed numbers by letters, and a Greek testament shows the employment of this method of expression by the Greeks also, as in Revelation xiv, 18, where the number 666 is written *Xsu.* Mackey's Masonic Encyclopedia refers to it under the head of "Alphabet."

The common origin of the two series is manifest in their agreement up to the letter P. The ancient employment of the decimal system (generally denied by scholars) is proved by the arrangements in digits, tens, and hundreds, and the greater antiquity of the Greek series by its agreement with Egyptian, Chaldaic and Hindu (Sanskrit) words, older than Hebrew.

The many qualities peculiar to numbers and the prevalence in Nature of forms answering to the figures of geometry caused many ancient philosophers to believe that the entire scheme of the universe was based upon mathematics. Those curious scientific playthings called "acrostics" and "magic squares" were looked upon as marvels of mystic meanings, during a bygone age.

Understanding this, we can translate into their proper number values the proportions, ground plans, and ornaments of ancient temples, besides countless biblical names and phrases, classic proper names, magic words, and above all the passwords of our Masonic craft which explain the acts and allusions that accompany them.

This is really what constituted the speculative Masonry of oldtime seers, and shows it to have been far beyond the mental reach of the illiterate stonecutters—to whom so many of our brethren love to ascribe the authorship of our fraternity.

This system was really based upon a 26-letter alphabet answering to the 26 of JHVH, of which *alpha* was the first letter, *mu* or *mem* the middle, and *omega* the last, philosophically referring to the beginning, middle, and end of human life.

The "nonary" system (derived from nine, or "3 times 3") is identical with what we now call the "decimal" system. The ancients, prior to the invention of the *Abacus,* employed a series of decimal places running from right to left, represented by shallow dishes or holes scooped in the sand. The empty hole represented zero (position without number). As soon as there were 10 pebbles or other counters in any hole, they were removed and one was placed in the decimal position to the left. By this means decimal computations up into the trillions were possible, with the precision of an adding machine. Certain numbers show the peculiarity of representing two different sacred quantities; as, for instance, the number 888. This has a special significance of its own, but was constructed from 3 times 8 (24) counters (8 units, 8 tens, and 8 hundreds)—there being a mystic relationship between the two ideas represented and between the two numbers involved.

To the brother who is really interested in learning the truth about this wonderfully constituted ritual of ours, it may be emphasized that failure to know or recognize these methods of the ancients has been the reason why so many of the past expounders of Masonry have failed to "hit the mark."

"Three Times Three"

No term throughout the entire range of Masonic symbolism so completely clenches the connection between Freemasonry and the Ancient Mysteries as this most important link. The number 9 is a part of the great harmony of the universe, and as such was recognized longer ago than man has history. A study of the peculiarities of this number will soon set at rest any wonder as to why it has secured such a paramount place in symbolism.

Nine—that is to say, the nine digits—is the basis of number, and therefore of time, space, and proportion, which cannot be expressed in any terms but those of numbers. The ancient number philosophy was the basis of every symbolic system of expressing the nature and attributes of Deity that the world has ever known. Even where important number symbols are

GEMATRIA

The numerical values represented, among the Ancients
by the letters of the Greek and Hebrew Alphabets.

GREEK and HEBREW (identical.)

A	B	G	D	H	U or V or O	Z	Ch
Aleph	Beth	Gimel	Daleth	Heh	Vau	Zain	Cheth
א	ב	ג	ד	ה	ו	ז	ח
1	2	3	4	5	6	7	8
Alpha	Beta	Gamma	Delta	Epsilon	Episemon*	Zeta	Eta
α	β	Γ, γ	Δ, δ	ε	ϛ	z	η

Th	Y or I or J	K	L	M	N	S	O (guttural)	P
Teth	Jod	Kaph	Lamed	Mem	Nun	Samech	Ayin	Peh
ט	י	כ	ל	מ	נ	ס	ע	פ
9	10	20	30	40	50	60	70	80
Theta	Iota	Kappa	Lambda	Mu	Nu	Xi	Omikron	Pi
θ	ι	κ	Λ, λ	μ	ν	Ξ ξ	o	Π π

HEBREW

Tz	Q	R	Sh	T	K	M
Tsaddi	Qoph	Resh	Shin	Tau	Final Kaph	Final Mem
צ	ק	ר	ש	ת	ך	ם
90	100	200	300	400	500	600

N	P	Tz	
Final Nun	Final Peh	Tsaddi	Dotted Aleph
ן	ף	ץ	א
700	800	900	1000

GREEK (and probably Egyptian)

Q	R	S	T	U	Ph
Kappa	Rho	Sigma	Tau	Upsilon	Phi
ϙ	P	Σ	T	Υ	Φ
90	100	200	300	400	500
η	ρ	σ or ς	τ	υ	φ

X	Ps	W		
Chi	Psi	Omega	Sanpi	Alpha dashed
X	Ψ	Ω		
600	700	800	900	1000
χ	ψ	ω	ξ	ϙ

*Episemon is often called Digamma

apparently independent of 9, it will be found that they are based thereon. Its connection with geometry is fundamental.

The archeological proofs that this system possessed no geographical limits, but was as common to Mound Builder, Aztec, and Inca as to Chaldean, Hebrew, Persian, Egyptian, Greek, Phenician, Mongol, Druid, and Hindu, are irrefutable. The symbols of "Three Times Three" among all these peoples are so much alike as at once to arrest the attention of the antiquarian.

It is well known that any number, great or small, multiplied by 9 will give a product the sum of whose digits will exactly equal nine. This mergence of everything into 9 was likened to consumption by fire,

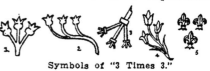

Symbols of "3 Times 3."

1, Babylonian and Hebrew (Aaron's rod); 2, early Greek; 3, ancient Guatemala; 4, lilies of the Virgin; 5, heraldic lilies.

which caused 9 to be termed the number of Vulcan, which latter name was derived from Tubal Cain, the Semitic "spirit of fire," that which resolves all that it attacks into its original elements.

Nine thus stands in the great old number philosophy as the representative of the primordial substance from which all emanated and to which all must eventually return. The remaining eight digits were accepted as the elements of the "dual principle," embracing positive and negative, spiritual and material, male and female, odd and even, etc. The spiritual or "male" numbers were the indivisible "odd" ones; while those representing matter, the female principle, were "even" and divisible.

Multiplying each of the first eight digits by 9 gives us 18, 27, 36, 45, 54, 63, 72, and 81, the sum of which is 396, a number greatly reverenced by ancient mystics because, among many reasons, added to the number 270, the period of human gestation in days, it produced the sacred 666, and indicated the incarnation of the solar *logos* in humanity.

From earliest times the letter M, with the value of 40, has been the mystical character of this incarnate "Word." In the Hindu triglyph A.U.M., in which the first, last, and middle letters of the sacred alphabet stand for Brahma, Shiva, and Vishnu, the creator, destroyer, and preserver, or "youth, old age, and manhood," M is the symbol of this preserving manifestation of Deity, whose material emblems are the lamb, the corn, and the vine, and is shown in connection with wheat-ears and grapes on the Syrian coins of B. C. 360, from the figure on which the Greeks copied their conception of Zeus or Jove, while it appears in various ways elsewhere, especially in the religious ornaments of the Byzantine Empire. In "Orient" Masonry the letter M is employed instead of G in connection with the square and compasses. The Manifested Word is the World Builder or Great Architect, the *Rab Bone* of the Essenes, or *Nazorim*, the Chaldean Seers (see Hebrews i, 1-3; St. John xx, 16). Another designation is that of the "Alpha and Omega," the two supplementary letters of A. U. M. (Revelation i, 8 *et seq.*)

Let us see where we now stand with regard to the connection with these particular circumstances of primitve Freemasonry.

The letter M (40) represents 396 because it is the sum of 18 and 22 *which multiplied together produce it*. The ancients made frequent use of words each letter of which was the initial of another word, the whole forming a sentence. Thus the Romans constructed from A. U. M. *Arcifex Universus Mundi*, or "Architect of the Universe of Worlds." The founders of our modern ritualistic formulas—even if they have given us no intimation—have at least left it for us to discover the use of the same formula in the term G. A. O. T. U., in which the letters G, T, U, respectively, are 3, 9, and 6, reducible to 40 or M, the remaining two being the *Alpha* and *Omega*.

We shall profit by one or two sage oriental reflections upon this wonderful figure 9. The "Nikita Karma," or Brahmin sacred book of occult science, says, "It is now time for the virtuous father who possess a son, over whose head has rolled *three times three* years, *the figure of the tutelary spirits,* to perform the ceremony of the *Oupanayana*" (introduction to the study of the liberal arts and sciences). "He should then contemplate the infinite perfection of Brahma. He should ponder the *Three Triads* which have sprung from Him and have created the 8,400,000 creatures, at the head of which is *man*."

The care of the sacred fire in the temples is always intrusted to nine Brahmans.

The ninefold constitution of the universe was set forth by the ancients as follows: Three forms of matter, gaseous, liquid, and solid; three forms of motion, from a center, to a center, round a center; three magnitudes of bodies, length, breadth, and thickness.

The great French Masonic mystic, Ragon, in writing of this expression, says, "If the number 'three' was greatly esteemed by the early sages, the number *three times three* has not been less celebrated, because, according to them, every one of the elements that go to make up our body is triple,—water containing both earth and fire, earth containing both igneous and aqueous particles, and fire being tempered by globules of water and earthly corpuscles, which serve as its food. As not one of these elements is thus ever found simple and without admixture of the others, all material beings, being composed of these three elements, each triple, can therefore be designated by the figurative number *three times three;* hence it became the symbol of incorporization. Hence also the name of 'ninefold envelop' given to matter.''

The Number "Seven"

All modern theology has its rise in the immeasurably old "number philosophy" of the ancient world.

The name *JAH* was given to our universe because it represented the number 16, which in turn was composed of 3+4=7 and 4+5 =9 (J=10, A=1, H=5). These two combinations are the two fundamental right angles of all geometry and the ones upon which most of our symbolisms are founded.

The astounding recurrence of the number 7, not only in geometrical figures, but in countless curious objects of human speculation, caused it to be regarded with superstitious awe. It was regarded as one of good augury because most of the things beneficial to mankind came in series of sevens. When the ancient star gazers had finally determined the planets of our universe (those, of course, discernible to the naked eye), each item of the numerous septenary sets conceived of by our forefathers was attributed to the influence of one of the planets, deemed the dwelling of a superior intelligence active for the good or ill of humanity.

Thus the seven planets were the seven old gods of the Babylonians,—Shamash, the Sun; Sin, the Moon; Nebo, Mercury; Ishtar, Venus; Nergal, Mars; Marduk, Jupiter; and Ea, Saturn.

The Jewish seven-branched candlestick and its symbolism.

They had other names as gods in nearly every oriental country. To the Hebrews they were the archangels Michael, Gabriel, Raphael, Samael, Uriel, Amiel, Zadkiel. To the early Christians they were the Angels of the Seven Churches. They were represented among the Jews, Babylonians, Egyptians, and Persians by seven branched candlesticks (*Menorah*) or seven-flamed altar fires.

A list of their supposed emanations would be almost interminable; but here are a few to go on with:

The seven vowels, primary colors, notes of music, metals, days of the week, liberal arts, rounds of the spiritual ladder or staircase, deadly sins, sorrows of the Virgin Mary; the seven rays or Heptaktis of Jao Sabaoth among the Chaldeans; the seven rays of Indra in Hindu Mythology; the seven stars of the Pleiades, in Taurus; the Seven Ages of Man, not invented by Shakespeare, but quoted by Solon, the Athenian lawgiver, and by the school of Hippocrates; the seven Hyades, the seven stars of the Great Bear, forming a Swastika, in which the Hindus placed their seven *Rishi* or sages of primitive wisdom; seven wonders of the world; seven reeds to Pan's pipe; seven strings to Apollo's Lyre; seven gifts of the Holy Ghost; seven champions of Christendom; seven sleepers of Ephesus; seven *Amshaspands* of Persian theology, and seven Heavens.

The number 7 times 7 was still more sacred, and seven seven-pointed stars ornament the collar of a Grand Master of Masons under the York rite.

Of course there are a hundred more considerations of this interesting number; but almost all may be traced to different racial speculations on the same themes, derived from the contemplation by the ancient Sabeans of the seven planets of our universe.

The "Pi" Proportion and Genesis

One of the finest examples of the application of the ancient number Philosophy, is to be found in the very first verse of the first chapter of Genesis, which reads as follows: "In the beginning God created the heavens and the earth," etc.

The Holy Bible, aside from the beautiful quality of the Elizabethan or rather Jacobean English of its translators, which rings so sweetly to the Anglo-Saxon ear, is not an English document. It is the best rendition that the best men of several periods have been able to give us, according to their best contemporary lights, of a Hebrew "Old Testament" and a Greek "New Testament."

As original documents, in their respective original tongues, there is no secret among scholars that the first reflects a great volume of Chaldean mysticism and that the second bears the impress of the schools of Alexandria. The Old Testament is the Holy Book of the Hebrews, and their scholarship has been concerned with it for some thousands of years, bearing fruit in that colossal commentary called the *Talmud* and the deeply mystical *Kabbalah*, not to speak of the profound and almost inspired writings of Philo Judæus.

The philosophical system known as that of the "Chaldean Numbers" is sufficiently in evidence in the works quoted to disprove any suspicion that they are an invention for the purpose of proving something connected with modern Masonry.

They are the basis of the so-called Pythagorean system, which sought to erect a complete theory of cosmogony on a mathematical basis, and we are now justified in believing that Pythagoras did no more than pass into Greece that which he learned from the hierophants of Chaldea and Central India.

Many Hebrews and Greeks employ the letters of their respective alphabets as numbers, to this very day.

Almost all the ancient names of Deity, when their letters are resolved into numbers, are found to consist of what are sometimes called "cosmic" numbers, in that they set forth some great and majestic planetary or terrestrial cycle which attests

41

the stupendous scope of divine power and wisdom. The "Ineffable" Name is the most remarkable of these cabalistic words, because it can be shown in various ways to be the pivotal formula upon which turned the seven primitive sciences of the Chaldeans. In the original texts there are over a dozen different names of Deity, which are uniformly translated "God," even though individually they possess shades of meaning conveying notions of special divine attributes.

The two accounts of Creation embodied in the book of Genesis are called the "Elohistic" and "Jehovistic," respectively, because of the employment of the distinct titles "ALHIM" and "JHVH."

The former, the letters of which are valued as 1-30-5-10-40, are quoted by Mme. Blavatsky as giving the *Pi* proportion when written in a circle. Arranged as an acrostic, however, in the 25 squares of Pythagoras' "square on the hypothenuse," and employing only the digits in the final expression (see illustration), the result is much better.

"Bezaleel, the builder of the Tabernacle in the Wilderness," says the Talmud, "knew the transposition of letters by which God created the World."

ALHIM, reversed into "MIHLA," is a Hebrew word expressing "circumcision." The addition of the digits of 3.1415 is 14, which was the value of the diameter of a circle in a wide range of oriental philosophies, because 3 1-7 times 14 is 44, or 11 x 11, the perimeter of which closely corresponds with that of a circle, 14 of the same parts in diameter. This problem is one of the most noted Egyptian hieroglyphs, and is profusely sculptured on the facade of the great Temple of Hathor at Denderah.*

The 3.1415 formula of the *Pi* proportion is popularly attributed to the noted Greek mathematician and engineer Archimedes of Syracuse.

It is not final, however, and the greatest and most painstaking of German mathematicians have continued the Archimedean

H	,	ם	א	ל
ל	ה	,	ם	א
א	ל	ה	,	ם
ם	א	ל	ה	,
,	ם	א	ל	ה

L	A	M	I	H
A	M	I	H	L
M	I	H	L	A
I	H	L	A	M
H	L	A	M	I

30	1	40	10	5
1	40	10	5	30
40	10	5	30	1
10	5	30	1	40
5	30	1	40	10

3	1	4	1	5
1	4	1	5	3
4	1	5	3	1
1	5	3	1	4
5	3	1	4	1

Elohim (Alhim) the "Pi" Proportion.

*See A∴ U∴ M∴ by Author.

process until they have run the figure into several score of decimal places without attaining finality. This is precisely what the ancient mind probably meant to express, with exquisite reverence—a creative factor inseparable from all orderly arrangement of matter, which could not be proved finite.

The verse that embodies "ALHIM" is—

In the beginning God (Elohim) created the Heaven and Earth, and the Earth was without form and void, etc.

It is completely in accord with the ancient philosophy, which, in apostrophizing the Deity as the "*Pi* proportion," meant what later, in Isaiah, is called "The living Elohim,"—The *Pi* proportion, endowed with omnipotent self-exertion in the ordering of inchoate matter; in other words, a LOGOS active in Cosmos. The *Pi* proportion is something that is never absent, in one form or other, from every one of the world's primitive religions, and certainly enters deeply and radically into the philosophies that have given rise to what we in these days call "Masonry."

Masonry in a Snowflake

As an example of the depth of which the Number Philosophy penetrates into the very heart of Nature, when geometrically considered, the study of a mere snow crystal affords us a striking object lesson.

The State of Vermont possesses a specialist in the microphotography of snowflakes. He is an enthusiast, who has collected many hundreds of photographs of newly fallen snowflakes by photographing them as they descend upon a sheet of black paper, in an open-air studio, through a purposely left aperture in the roof.

His pictures make manifest that the snowflake is, in a sense, during its ephemeral career, a living organism, in that it, while seemingly possessed of myriad crystalline forms, follows a definite law of development, from the most primitive geometrical figure, a perfect equilateral triangle, to a gorgeous foliate crystal of many points or ''buds.''

Direct Photographs of Snow Crystals.

The fundamental circumstances seem about as follows: When the chemical atoms of oxygen and hydrogen encounter and combine as moisture in the presence of a sufficiently low temperature to congeal as they do so, an ice crystal is formed, the geometrical character of which is governed by the ultimate globular

44

structure of its molecules. Now, it is demonstrable that equilateral triangles and hexagons are the only perfect geometrical figures that may be used to divide masses of spheres or circles, in closest possible contact, into symmetrical groups. Hence the electricity of the atmosphere, which at once finds lodgment upon all particles of moisture in suspension (whence the phenomena of lightning and thunder also), becomes the life force of the newly formed drop, and manifests its dynamic power equally in every direction; but always in straight lines, divergent from other straight lines *at angles of 60 degrees.*

The result is a fixed visualization of the electric spark which for the moment has clothed itself in the aqueous fluid, obedient only to the molecular constitution of the latter. The elaborateness of the resultant design is evidently dependent on the strength of the electric charge and the volume of water acted upon; the innumerable photographs taken through a powerful microscope reveal no variations in the law of progress.

The miracle of the thing lies in the fact that in the center of each of these beautiful six-pointed ice flowers is revealed the hexagonal star that the ancient Hindu occultists united in proclaiming the symbol of fire (or spirit), the up-pointed triangle, and water (matter) the down-pointing triangle. In India this figure is the united seal of Vishnu and Shiva, or "Life and Death," intimately associated in metaphysics with "Spirit" and "Matter." It is also one of the principal emblems of Scottish Rite Masonry and of the Theosophical Society.

Among our Hebrew brethren this sacred symbol is called the *Mogun Dovid,* or "Shield of David," and also the "Seal of Solomon." It is embroidered in gold on the veil that conceals the sacred scroll of the Law in the Tabernacle. It is stamped in gold on the cover of the Jewish Bible, surmounts the spires of synagogues, and is a universal emblem throughout the Mohammedan world.

The larger flake selected for illustration (both are from unretouched negatives) exhibits 13 "buds" to each of its six points, resulting in the ancient Hebrew cabalistic number 78, which stood for HIH HVVH VIHIH ("He that Was—He that Is—He who is to come" or "Ever shall be").

The other figure is a less developed specimen, which displays a single perfect down-pointing equilateral triangle, the geometrical value of which is like that of all triangles, the sum of the angles of which is 180 degrees, or a semicircle. This in Hebrew cabalism was S (60) L (30) M (40) N (50), while in the center are displayed three little circles like the letter O. The symbol therefore reads "S o L o M o N."

This is by no means the end of the series of beautiful cabalistic mysteries attached to these exquisite natural figures; but it must indeed convey an inspiring thought to our Jewish brother to reflect that every flake of pure, white, driven snow that has fallen from heaven to earth during the eons of time that separate us from creation has carried as its divine message this beautiful emblem of his race and faith, so much of which is indissolubly riven to the Masonic craft.

Yet there are still to be found many brethren who will tell us glibly, "There are no mysteries in Masonry"!

Mohammedan Copper Coin of Morocco.

King Solomon's Temple

In our F. C. degree is embodied far more particular reference to the subject of Israel's great and world-famous Temple than in either the preceding or the following degrees. Indeed, upon strict analysis, the F. C. degree serves as little more than a fitting prelude and climax to the soul-stirring imagery of the M. C. lecture, which Masons have ever united in declaring to be the most beautiful and impressive allocution in our entire ritual.

It was undoubtedly the work of an author of profound culture, possessed of deep insight into the ancient mysteries; for it contains many allusions to facts long since relegated to oblivion in a language the very ingenuousness of which is a marvelous subtlety, and, while seemingly but a relation of prosaic historical facts, is in reality one of the greatest metaphysical documents in the language of any time or place.

The three principal contemplations of the ancient philosophical mind were God, the Universe, Man. The supreme science of the universe viewed physical, Man as at once the Temple of God and the home of spiritual Man; thus investing the human individual with the same responsible stewardship that any master might reasonably exact from the servant, whose duty it was to keep his residence pure and undefiled.

The teaching of salutary truths has ever been best accomplished, according to Oriental ideas, in the form of picturesque allegories and imageries which take hold upon the imaginations of the young and serve an admirable purpose in fixing upon the mind important truths, dissimulated to the "profane," but intense in meaning and purpose to the initiate. The sacred books of the world have all without exception been composed with this end in view.

Ask the time-occupied, busy, average Mason if he believes every word of the thrilling story with which he is made so familiar in the Lodge. He will frankly tell you no. "Part of it," he will say, "is true," because he can point to the literary source from which it is taken. "The rest," he will tell you, "may not be historically precise; but it is invaluable because of its efficiency in driving home and clenching the necessary moral lesson."

In these words he will be uttering a perfect description of

the method pursued by the moral teachers of the ancient world, practically without exception. The western world is densely oblivious of the fact that a vast system of dissimulation of natural truths was begun at a remote date, by the priestly caste. Multitudes were unable to seize the idea of "reality" upon a purely spiritual plane. They could grasp only with the senses, just as the education in liberality of very young children begins with Santa Claus, who later proves to be "only Papa."

The considerations involved are too extensive to be adequately treated in a short commentary. They cover almost the entire domain of philosophy and metaphysics; but we venture a thought or so that may be helpful to the reverent seeker after "more light" who hesitates to enter the door of initiation because of a highly commendable fear that he may be taking a plunge into some unrealized profanation.

We need have no moral compunction about rereading the secular histories of most of the ancient nations, as those transmitted to us by the Greek historians of the Ptolemaic and Selucid periods of Egypt and Syria are shown by modern research to have been glaringly inaccurate as to the details of persons and events, although still carrying enough of such truth as had become traditional, to have a corroborative value in instances. The scholarship of the last century has recovered so much of the genuine history of the classic peoples, from their own records and monuments, as completely to destroy the value of those fantastic compilations (Berosus and Manetho, for instance) upon which many early 19th century biblical commentaries were constructed.

The entire pantheons of the ancient culture nations were composed of the attributes or emanations of a single, unrevealed, omnipotent Deity, considered as "Intelligences," and therefore possessing a species of individual Ego, controlled by the great central Power.

These divine intelligences were, for more complete realization, distributed throughout the solar system, when the incessant revolution and ever changing aspects of the latter became the basis of a great cosmic drama, so that the loves and hates, the wars and friendly gatherings, of the "gods" (*Elohim*) might be described in anthropomorphisms, or terms pertaining to the affairs of men. The initiate alone, through all the ages, possessed the key to this sacred science of secrecy, and stood in the breach between the untutored masses and their superstitious regard for the powers of Nature.

Generation upon generation of ancient hierophants knew that by "Hercules" was meant the planet Mercury at the moments of its numerous passages through the Solar corona, at which periods it became draped in the lion's skin; yet they constructed an elaborate genealogy for the kings of Macedon which shows them to have been lineally descended from Hercules and Dejanira. Similar pedigrees were enjoyed by all the monarchs of old, especially the Egyptian Pharaohs, who were all sons of the sun god *Ra,* so that the analogous claims of the emperors of China and Japan in our own day are not without ample precedent. Alexander the Great of Macedon is always shown on his coins and monuments wearing a lion's skin as headdress, in honor of this peculiar parentage.

With reference to this widespread system of mystic theology, two facts may be established by any careful student.

The ever-recurrent course of universal nature being the basis upon which all arguments, however picturesque, are erected, the details are everywhere the same.

The sacred vocabularies of western peoples are mainly composed of translations and corruptions of eastern names and terms, largely Phenician and Egyptian, showing the direction traveled.

The earliest known historical mention of the Jewish people, on a monument of King Shishank.

In our western world we have the completed spiritual edifice of our own Great Light, sufficing for all our present needs; but it also has its archeology, and those few of us who have the time and patience to go back and delve into what are commonly called the "Fathers of the Church" and into the grand old *Talmud* of Israel, and even do not stop until we reach the rude symbols of spiritual insight away back in the Bronze Age, are rewarded by the view of an infinity of constructive material which the hand of Time has cleared away,—the rubbish of our Temple.

It has been necessary to dwell upon these details in order to make manifest the process by which living men became mythical heroes and their memories draped in the splendors of the universe. Man was endowed with a threefold constitution. His soul was a spark of the unrevealed Divinity, his spirit was bestowed upon him by the particular planet under the influence of which, according to the astrologer, he entered the realm of matter, while his body was an accretion of the elements, suspended in zones between the earth and the heavens. Thus the very kingship of the King determined his identity with the Sun, and his panegyrists did not hesitate so to blend the human and divine, the natural and supernatural, that we are today speechless in wonder before the more than remarkable character of Solomon, the Sun King—a character historical without doubt, but elaborated upon until its glory has extended to the "uttermost parts of the earth."

We have, during the last century, recovered the entire and unbroken chronology of the Assyrian and Babylonian monarchies. The records of these ancient peoples consist in several instances of complete libraries made up of thousands of clay tablets, containing not only tradition and history, extending back to approximately B. C. 4500, verified by accounts of astronomical phenomena occurring in different reigns, by which modern savants are able to fix dates to the very hour and minute, but also dictionaries, works on mathematics, syllabaries, by which the dead Sumerian and Akkadian writings could be translated into Babylonian, and elaborate records of the dealings of the kings of these countries with surrounding nations.

In not one single instance is there the slightest trace or track of an allusion to either a Hebrew nation prior to B. C. 925, or kings named David and Solomon at all.

According to the Hebrew record, these monarchs flourished about B. C. 1000-1100, which would render them contemporary with Kings Marduk-Nadin-Akhi, Marduk-Shapik-Zerim, and Ramman-apil-iddina of the first Babylonian empire and Tiglath-Pileser I, Shamshi-Ramman I, and Ashur-Bel-Kala of Assyria. As to Egypt, the biblical Solomonic period lies parallel to that of the later Ramesside kings of Thebes, and precedes that of Shishank of Bubastis, whose inscription on the walls of the great Temple of Karnak, including the "King of Judah" among the list of his prisoners in an expedition, is the first secular reference to the latter people. This king is presumed to have been Rehoboam, whose father and grandfather were the individual monarchs immortalized under the names of "David" and "Solomon." Jehu, king of Israel in the reign of King Shalmanesar II, of Assyria, was the first biblical monarch whose name was actually recorded on a contemporary monument (B. C. 800). It is a long forgotten fact that all the ancient Hebrew names, beginning with the ineffable *Tetragrammaton,* are cabalistic constructions, upon a system borrowed from the Chaldeans, who were an equally Semitic people and the rootstock of the Abramic tribes.

Not only was each of the 22 letters of the Hebrew alphabet a number, so that geometrical and mathematical formulas expressed in letters became words, but the three Hebrew letters A, Z, and J represented the elements earth, water, and fire respectively; Ch, V, H, Th, L, M, N, S, O, Tz, Q, Sh, the 12 signs of the zodiac, beginning with *Aries*, and G, B, D, K, P, R, T, the *Menorah* or Saturn, Jupiter, Mars, Sun, Venus, Mercury, and the Moon. Thus all the possible astronomical aspects of the heavens either spelled words already known or suggested new ones.

Where Science and Theology Met.
A Druidical Stone Circle.

The name "Solomon" is as completely cabalistic as the powers attributed to the great founder of our craft; but it antedates its use as that of Israel's king, for we have a king of Assyria at B. C. 1300 named Shalmanesar, the construction of whose name, from "S—L—M—N" and the word "*sar*," meaning "king," is as unequivocally "King Solomon" as the latter in English.

Why then were these letters employed? No one can fail to find them aligned in the Hebrew alphabet, as representative of the values 60, 30, 40, 50, the sum total of which is 180, or the semicircle of the sun's daily journey from east to west and nightly voyage through the underworld from west to east. It also represents the passage of the sun from the sign of Leo the lion, through Virgo, Libra, Scorpio, and Sagittarius, causing it to describe the *Royal Arch,* of which Libra, the highest of the 12 signs, constituted the *Keystone* from B. C. 1835 to A. D. 325. This passage, through five signs, constitutes the completion of each year's symbolic Temple to the Author and Giver of All

Good, represented by the element "Fire," the Earth sign Taurus (corresponding to the letter A as well as V—*Aleph,* an Ox) and two signs of Gemini in each case suggesting the analogy between Hercules and Apollo (*Tammuz* or *Adonis*) of later eschatology, and *the two sons of David,—Jedediah* ("God's Strength") and *Adonijah* ("God's Love"). Hercules, as the Tyrian Melkarth (*Melek-Kartha*), was *Hermes* "King of the City" (of Tyre), and Apollo *Hermes,* the Divine Wisdom, who accompanies the Sun, the nearest of all his planetary retinue, until in pursuance of the divine order the planet Mercury "falls" in this thrice yearly circuit about the Lord of Day as the latter passes the sign of Libra, the highest of the 12.

The story of Solomon and his Temple is not a mere chronicle of historical events, but, employing actual events and personages of far less contemporary historical importance than represented, as the basis of fact, the transcendent literary and spiritual genius of Israel wove a marvelous fabric of Oriental splendor, the object of which was to display the glory of Jehovah in His Universe in such a manner as indelibly to impress it upon the minds of men for all time.

The symbolization of the Universe by means of a Temple edifice may be traced in the earliest Mesopotamian monuments. They were originally conceived as gigantic sun-dials constituted by erecting a circle of 12 upright stones around a central altar. These were the ancient Palestinian *gilgals* and were the patterns for the later Druidical circles. A study of their shadows enabled the priests to predict the changes in the seasons, knowledge extremely useful to agricultural and pastoral peoples. As time passed and knowledge increased, the forms of religious edifices were made to express this developed science. Their masses were outlined in angles which recorded the direction of the plane of the ecliptic, the earth's axis, and the equator, the elevation above the horizon of the polar star, and constellations heralding the equinoxes and solstices.

Far antedating the Pyramids of Egypt were the step pyramids or seven-storied zigurrats, as the Temple observatories were called among the Assyrians, Babylonians, and Chaldeans. They did not embody all the details of the Hebrew description, but they were the original "King Solomon's Temples."

The Working Tools of E. A.

Our lodge is in every respect a symbolic workshop, furnished with all the tools belonging to the different grades of workmen, and with a trestleboard upon which are set forth the day's designs and the material upon which the labor of the brethren is to be expended.

This symbolic material consists of the two ashlars, emblematic of the crude material and the finished product, which are placed plainly enough on view in New York lodges, but absent or almost unknown, except to students, in many other states. The oblong stones and nondescript slabs sometimes seen are noteworthy evidence that the age-old significance of the "cubical stone," which has played such a prominent role in the mythology and mysticism of the past, has almost run to oblivion in the modern craft. These stones should really be perfect cubes. The symbolism of the working tools is completely lost the moment such proportions are lost sight of or ignored.

The ancient Hebrews had their own version of the great "number philosophy," which lent sanctity and expressiveness to the number 12. First of all, it was the number of their Twelve Tribes, who were doubtless a symbolical enrolment of all the heads of families under the zodiacal sign of the month in which they were born. It is certainly significant that the patriarchal system was founded upon this number, and later on many other dispositions were made that showed a particular reverence for the Chaldean plan of the universe based upon 12 signs. As one cube possesses six sides, each of which is a perfect square, a number of remarkable mathematical and geometrical symbolisms were established based upon the fact that all the numbers, from one to 12 added together produce 78. This number is also the sum of 3 times "26," the numerical value of the "Great and Sacred Name of Jehovah" (JHVH).

As each cube possesses 12 edges, the combined number require a 24-inch rule to symbolize their total outline. The breaking into different mathematical combinations of this supreme number, each significant of some one of the great ruling phenomena of nature, was seen in the symbolism of the use of an operative Mason's gavel in the dressing of building stones.

The grand mystery name of our Creator, called the *Tetragrammaton* (Greek for "four-letter name") had as its root the three letters J, H, and V, which as numbers were 10, 5, and 6, or 21, the sum of the added numbers 1 to 6 represented by a single cube. This was the form of the "Holy of Holies," in the great Temple of Solomon and the pious Jew, to this day, employs the two symbolic cubes, in the form of *Phylacteries*.

This fact was made the basis of a curious legend, wrought by the wise old rabbis into that marvelous compilation called the Talmud, from which more than a little of our Masonic material has been derived.

The story is of the Patriarch Enoch (Hanok, father of Methuseleh), whose name means "the initiator," who, all accounts agree, lived 365 years, or a "year of years." A remarkable book attributed to him is often alluded to by the Hebrew commentators and early Christian "Fathers"; but no trace of it was ever found until in the last century it turned up in Abyssinia. It has been translated out of that strange African dialect into many tongues. The so-called Book of Enoch contains a remarkable recital of astronomical science as known to the ancients, told entirely in allegorical form, while the history of the Children of Israel is prophesied (?) under the allegorical simile of the remarkable doings of a singularly intelligent flock of sheep which build a house for their shepherd, the whole reading very much like a children's fairy tale.

The Talmudic legend of Enoch represents him as greatly disturbed at the news of the impending world "Deluge," for fear the Name of God should be lost. He accordingly caused it to be inscribed upon a triangular plate of gold, and affixed it to a cubical stone, for the safe keeping of which he caused a series of nine arched vaults to be constructed, one beneath another, at the foot of Mt. Moriah (the holy mountain of the Jews, as Mt. Meru was of the Hindus). The rains came and the flood descended, and so washed the mud and silt over the site that it became completely obliterated.

Centuries later, when King David was moved "to build an house unto the Lord," and actually set his workmen to dig the foundations thereof, the latter discovered the vaults, and descending therein brought to light the long-buried stone.

Tradition also has it that the material of this stone was agate, which would at once connect it with the Hermetic philosophy; for agate, above all, was sacred to Hermes and Thoth or David. The latter, having been a warlike monarch, was not permitted to achieve that which he had begun and so bequeathed the *cubical stone* to his son Solomon, who made use of it as the cornerstone of the Temple.

The imagery of this is plain enough in the fact that, not in a written or engraved inscription, but in the mathematical proportions of the cube itself, was to be found that wonderful Name which is, as it were, the foundation of the universe, of which man is a fleshly epitome and the Temple on Mt. Moriah a symbolic one.

By knowing the use of the working tools of an E. A. the initiate might begin his labor of hewing and shaping the brute matter at his feet into stones fit for the builders' use; but when he had accomplished his task he was apprised that the symmetry and order it represented in its finished shape was "God": not a god whom he had created, but a God whom his patient labor had revealed.

The cube itself was an age-old symbol of the spiritual Man, as set forth in the *Mahabarata* of ancient India:

A portion of Mine own Self, transformed in the world of life into an immortal Spirit, draweth round itself the senses of which the Mind, which is the Sixth, veiled in Matter.

Therefore we find the cube present in all the ancient mythologies, which were but racial cloaks for one and the same wisdom religion, understood by the priests of all countries alike as a symbol of the sixth sign of the zodiac, the characters portraying the great Mother of Wisdom and her divine son Man.

It is the task of the apprentice to break through the shell of matter and liberate the Divine Word that dwells within by opening his own spiritual perceptions to the light of the *Logos*. As the priceless statutes of Phidias and Praxiteles were once shapeless masses of unmeaning stone and the Parthenon a sea-worn crag, until gavel and gauge, mallet and chisel, in the hand of inspiration had performed their tasks, so has always been the lesson of the cube in its unshapen and shapen forms to the apprentice Mason.

The Middle Chamber

We know not how old or whence emanated the ritual of Freemasonry, but we do know that when we are in search of historical parallels to almost any of its allusions we must lose ourselves in a past so distant that we can only wonder at the fidelity with which certain traditions have been preserved. However much we owe to the Biblical account of Israel's great monarch and his splendid achievements in art, letters, and statesmanship, he is the subject of innumerable Oriental traditions, which are unknown to Holy Writ and connect his name with a wide range of associations outside the classic ones to which we are most accustomed.

His triple name of Sol-Om-On we derive from the Septuagint, which was a translation of the Hebrew sacred books into Greek, accomplished by a commission of learned Alexandrian rabbis sent to Jerusalem for the purpose by King Ptolmey Philadelphus with the aid of a commission appointed by the then High Priest Eleazar, about B. C. 246. These men were not only talented scribes, but were skilled in the secret science of their day, so that they were able to translate this wonderful old name back into the same form in which it had been revered among the Chaldean mystics for many centuries previously.

Irrespective of its application to a historical character, the name "Solomon" was a cabalistic composition intended profoundly to symbolize Divine Wisdom. The outward form of the name expressed precisely the same symbolism as the three principal officers of the Masonic lodge,—the sun rising in the east (Sol), the sun at meridian in the south (Om), and setting in the west (On). These three names, taken separately, were also very old, and in a variety of ways connected all that men had discovered of the wonders of the universe, showing that they were but varying aspects of the great Jehovah.

The discoveries of learned travelers, especially American savants connected with the University of Pennsylvania, have established the facts beyond doubt that Jehovah was worshiped centuries before the time of Abraham by the Mesopotamian peoples, and the Divine Wisdom (Sol-Om-On), recorded in the Babylon cuneiform inscriptions as *Salmanu*, with the word *Sar*

The great Temple of Bel at Borsippa opposite Babylon, with its seven
planetary Stages.

or King added, when the name was used as that of a monarch. We get it in our histories translated into Shalmanesar, and the Hebrews alliterated it into *Sar-Shalom* or Prince of Peace.

Without entering upon the curious considerations that, from what are really most interesting mathematical puzzles, produced these famous names, the Solomons of Babylonia actually possessed Temples dedicated to Divine Wisdom, which were schools of instruction in the arts and sciences, having as the final assembly hall of the priestly initiates a Middle Chamber reached by seven successive steps or stages.

The remains of a number of these old Wisdom Temples, of which the Biblical Tower of Babel was one of the principal, have been found in ruinous condition and buried in the debris of their fallen summits until the whole, prior to excavation, presented the aspect of shapeless mounds.

It was the belief of these ancient peoples that all things affecting humanity were governed by the planets, and so all things mundane were arranged as far as possible in series of *seven* so as to put each one under the rulership of a different planet.

The Temples in question resembled a nest of boxes, in that they were square edifices placed one upon the other on a diminishing scale. Their disposition from the bottom up was that of the planets in their respective order of velocity. Saturn, the slowest, was represented at the bottom by a black chamber;

Ancient Babylonians engaged in ceremonies relating to the Magian worship of the heavenly bodies. The crossed hands of the assemblage are in token of adoration of the Sun, Moon and Zodiac.—(From contemporary sculptures.)

then came an orange-hued Temple for Jupiter, then a red one for Mars. Above this was the Temple of the Sun covered with plates of gold, then that of Venus, of a pale yellow color, and the last of the initiations took place in the literally *Blue* Lodge, dedicated to the planet Mercury, of whom the old rituals told us that the three lesser lights were "the Sun, Moon, and Mercury." Above this was the silver-covered Temple of the Moon god, where the fully initiated hierophant took his place among the astronomers who studied the heavenly bodies from this elevated Middle Chamber.

Ancient sculptures remain, showing various orders of neophytes in such reverent attitudes that we are unable to wonder when we behold other scenes from the vicinity of these old Temples, in which the dramatic action of some of our most intimate degree work is shown with fidelity and spirit.

The Dedication of The Lodge

There is no more interesting series of incidents attached to any of the allusions of our Masonic ritual than that which links the tutelary guardianship of the lodge to the Holy Saints John.

Jonah, the original "Holy St. John."

The many Masonic references to these venerated patrons certainly call for clearer definition that we receive either from ritual or monitor, and naturally direct our minds to the questions of why their names should be applied to the lodge at all, the origin of the name itself, the association that we so continually encounter in Masonic symbolism of the two Saints John with the two parallel lines, one on each side of the point within the circle, and finally the descent of this symbolism from anterior forms, if any can be traced.

Laying aside all detail for the specialist, we must consider the enormous volume of substitution that was found necessary by the early church to adapt time-honored pagan rites and ceremonies to the new order.

When the Ancient Mysteries were taken under the protection of the Roman hierarchy and diverted into the channels that have led up to their preservation in their present form of Freemasonry, it was probably deemed expedient to replace the characters of the two Hermes by others more in keeping with the new faith. Thus, all the Masonic applications of the two Saints John may be found in the ancient employments of the planet Mercury as a Mystery symbol.

The ancient Babylonian pyramid temples of seven steps or stages, although each stage was dedicated to a different planet, were generally consecrated, like the great Babylonian Temple at Borsippa, to the god Nebo, who is this same alternate morning and evening star.

The temples of the Phenicians, especially the great prototype of King Solomon's Temple at Tyre, were dedicated to the two Hermes under the names of Baal and Melkarth, or Apollo and Hercules, to whom were sacred the two most critical moments of the year, the solstices.

The two parallel lines of Masonic symbolism are nothing more nor less than hieroglyphs of the pillars of the porch, while the point within the circle is the most ancient emblem of both the sun and the metal gold, symbolic of the sun's light. They were also often represented by two serpents or two fishes, moving in opposite directions.

As the axis of our earth is always comparatively vertical to the ecliptic, as we travel on our annual course round the sun, the ancients, who knew this from observations, symbolized it by erecting 12 vertical pillars or dolmens round a central altar fire, representing the sun. These were the earliest places of initiation; but as their principal use was to locate the precise moment of the solstices by their

Egyptian Scarabs four to five thousand years old, showing importance of the symbol of the two fishes.

shadows, as temples grew more architectural and ornate, only the solstice pillars were preserved and dedicated to Hermes. This must have been done, when the sign of Virgo, the "Day House" of Mercury, stood for the great Mother of Nature, as from B. C. 6155 to 3995, the earth was in this sign, and the sun in the opposite sign of the Fish at the winter solstice, while, at the summer solstice, the reverse obtained.

It is curious that the name of "John" should conduct us to this very circumstance; for it is a derivation from the age-old name of Oannes (*Ea-Han*), the name given by the Ninevites to this same planet Mercury, who, thrown out of the ship (falling below the sun as the latter passed through the sign of the Fish), disappeared, only to rise again triumphantly and become a teacher of men. The uncovered ruins of Nineveh are everywhere carved with colossal statutes of Oannes the Fish-man, whose tradition, as the first instructor of men in the arts and sciences, reached the Tyrians as that of Dag-On, "The fish of the Setting sun," and the Hebrews as *Jonh* (translated "Jonas" or "Jonah"). As the ancients saw the sun nightly sink in the west, far beyond the Straits of Gibraltar, they called the two promontories that flank it the "Pillars of Hercules"; by which names they are still known. The calabistic meaning of Jonh is *Jod; Vau, Heh;* and the letter *Nun,* which means *"a Fish."*

The Egyptian also dedicated twin pillars to Osiris and Isis, the signs of Leo and Virgo, whose son Horus is but another form of Hermes. They called that of Osiris "Strength" because it represented the power of God—which is "Hercules" again. The pillar of Isis they designated "Establishment," which referred to Nature, that which is set up and maintained by God's power, whose husband-son is the alternately dying and reviving divinity.

Among the Hebrews the sign of Isis, Virgo, the widow of Osiris and mother of Horus, was of the tribe of Naphtali, while the sign of Gemini was the tribe of Levi, from which sprang the two brothers Moses the warrior and lawgiver, and Aaron the High Priest, equally representative of the dual principle for which the two Hermes stood,—spirit and matter, the divine and the mortal.

So the two Holy Saints John, the one purely material and the other purely spiritual, were taken by Christian symbolists to personify the age-old Mystery of regeneration.

The symbol of the two fish, as they appear both among the Chinese and ancient Peruvians.

The Pillars of The Porch

The employment of twin pillars or posts at the threshold of edifices dedicated to religious purposes is a usage of the greatest antiquity. Even the original intention of church steeples was not expressed in a single one. as we so often see today. but in two, as the latter had once the same significance as the pillars.

A great volume of literature has attempted to give the pillars a purely phallic significance; but the writer has found many reasons for believing this to be an exaggeration.

Among all primitive peoples a pillar erected in the center of a convenient open space served as a *gnomon*, through which the daily, monthly, and annual aspects of the sun might be taken account of. The interpretation of the shadows cast by this pillar developed into quite a science, and was always the principal occupation of the priestly caste, who learned thereby to predict the approach and departure of the seasons correctly, thus making their wisdom indispensable to the pastoral and agricultural peoples whom they served. On the day of the summer solstice, at noon, when the sun stood vertically overhead, the Peruvians said that their god "sat upon his pillar."

As experiment succeeded experiment, perhaps over many centuries, it was discovered that a far greater range of solar phenomena could be registered through comparison of the shadows of two of these pillars, placed at some distance apart. All of these discoveries were kept locked within the breasts of the erudite priesthoods and constituted the real secrets that our ancient brethren were pledged, under fearsome penalties, to keep and conceal among the initiates of their own peculiar orders.

Many ancient Temple courts were paved with a pattern of alternate white and colored tiles, like a chessboard, over spaces carefully measured so as to extend "one-third longer from west to east than from north to south."

The two pillars or obelisks (the latter the favorite forms in Egypt) were placed at the northeast and southeast corners of this paved work so that when the sun rose on the morning of the summer solstice, it rose apparently in the northeast corner of the universe (which for other reasons was also considered as an oblong, 3 x 4 in dimensions) and the shadow of the corresponding pillar cut the court diagonally; thus describing the hypothenuse of the Pythagorean triangle (3—4—5), which was dedicated to Horus in Egypt, Bel in Chaldea, and Baal in Phenicia and Syria, all the same god of fertility and increase as well as patron of the liberal arts and sciences.

Phoenician stele of B.C. 1000, showing pillars, lily and pomegranate.

All these ideas are embodied in the reproduction of a Punic *stele* (Phenician monument) now preserved in the Bibliotheque Nationale of Paris. The human hand with extended fingers symbolized this number 5. The lily on one side was an emblem of Astarte or Isis, and the pomegranate, which, aside from the exuberance of its seed, exhibits as a transverse section a five-pointed star, an additional symbol of the Baal below, seen soaring between the pillars.

With this picture we are able to contrast the well-known Masonic symbol of the point-within-the-circle between the two parallels, which is nothing less than a hieroglyph of the foregoing figure. The sun, either as a plain or winged disk or represented by one of the various Baal or Horus figures of the ancients, is supposed to be seen at a distance from between the two pillars, just as the resplendent letter in the end of the lodge room would appear from the preparation room.

The eventual location of these twin pillars, in the west, arose from several causes. By the time the astronomical lore of the Chaldeans was ready to migrate to western Europe under the name of Druidism (the Druid priests were still called *Culdees* in Ireland), it had been ascertained that the axis of the earth always maintained a semi-erect position during its migration round the sun, and the ecliptic had been divided into the 12 equal parts or signs, corresponding to our months, that still obtain. This was symbolized everywhere by circles of 12 erect stones, with a fire altar in the center to symbolize the sun.

The pillars of the west have ever marked the scene of the
nightly tragedy of the loss of light and the annual one of the
death of nature. They are termed the Pillars of Hercules because of the scene of the descent into Hades which constituted
the last of the "12 labors" of this ancient year-god. His very
name of *Hr-akleos* shows him to have been the "ignoble,"
"poor," "needy," or "unfortunate" Hermes, also typified by
the blind Samson (*Shamash-On*) who precipitated the destruction of the lords of the Philistines, by seizing the pillars against
which he leaned. The two promontories, Gibraltar and Ceuta,
marking the westernmost extension of Europe,
were called the "Pillars of Hercules" by the
Phenecian sailors, and their symbol has, through
a variety of associations, become our American
dollar mark ($) of today.

The globe tops of the pillars represent in-
differently "heaven and earth" or the "sun and
moon," through an esoteric or hidden meaning
which has accompanied them from their original home in northern India.

The special allusion is to the "dual prin-
ciple," in which the right-hand column repre-   The Parallels.
sents *Purusha*, the male principle, and *Prakriti*,
the female principle, of human nature, worked out on a mathematical basis.

There is no possibility of present-day belief that these pillars
originated with the construction of any King Solomon's Temple
at Jerusalem. They are represented on too many monuments of
far greater age for this to be the case. In Tyre they stood before
the great temple of Melkarth, the Tyrian Hercules (Hiram, King
of Tyre). In Egypt they represented Osiris (strength) and Isis
(establishment). An Egyptian amulet in the writer's possession
shows the Egyptian god Bes, representing Osiris, as the Syrian
Baal approaching from the east through the two pillars, his head
surmounted by the three plumes that symbolized the letter G—
this also being an age-old cabalism, and not a modern symbol as
many suppose. The Egyptians also called these pillars the "Pillars of Set" or Typhon, with reference to the western Hades of
which we have already spoken.

Finally, the true Hebrew spellings of these pillars are
"IKIN" and BOAZ, which words, to be properly understood,
must be halved into IK-IN and BO-AZ, translated into their

numerical equivalents, 30-60 and 72-8. When multiplied together, the first will give 1,800 and the second 576; which, again multiplied, give 1,036,800, the precise length of 10 Hindu *Kali-Yugas* or great cycles in solar years and a number of other wonderful facts connecting the *Sod,* or secret doctrine of Israel, with the ancient Hindu *gnosis;* while the digits 3, 6, 7, 2, and 8 of the two words added together produce 26, or *Jod, Heh, Vau, Heh.*

Behold the W. M.
B. C. 2500.

The Lodge Room Floor

The old monitorial rescript concerning the correct form of the Masonic lodge will be found, greatly elaborated upon, in Mackey's Masonic Encyclopedia. It states that the room should be in the shape of a parallelogram or "oblong square," *at least* one-third larger from east to west than it is from north to south.

Scarabæus bearing signature of Thothmes III. B.C. 1503

We are elsewhere told that it should be "as high as the heavens and as deep as the surface from the center," likewise that it is "a representation of the universe on a reduced scale."

Few of us who encounter these random phrases are aware of how literally true they are and how full of the true spirit of ancient Masonry. Take, for instances, a plane surface *one-third longer than it is wide*. Geometrically it can mean only one thing, —a square composed of nine small squares to which three are added, making twelve, or an oblong three by four.

It may comes as a surprise, but this figure, next to the cube, was the most sacred one of the ancient world. It is almost always imperfectly and incorrectly represented by the paved mosaic oblong of "haphazard" dimensions, occupying the center of many of our lodge room floors, upon which the symbol of a "blazing star" is shown, with the altar in the center.

Oblongs of these precise dimensions are found all over the world,—among the amulets profusely strewn, in the mummy cases and wrappings of their dead, by the ancient Egyptians, and in the burial mounds of the long vanished American races that once dwelt from the Dakotas to the Andes.

Scarabæus with signature of Rameses II. B. C. 1330.

In its association with the lodge room, however, the exact relation of this particular figure to the language used in describing the former is that an elliptical line, exactly circumscribed within it, was taken by the ancient Egyptians, who made crude observations of the changes in the sun's apparent diameter and direction from the earth, from day to day, as the correct form of the orbit of our earth. It was the astronomer Kepler who is supposed to have discovered the laws of the planetary orbits, late in the 16th century. There is a host of detail connected with these laws of Kepler which prove that the relations of the heavenly bodies are following the precise mathematical laws of geometry; not at random, but eternally, with the same precision.

Kepler found it to be true that all the planets move in elliptical orbits round the sun, which is placed in one of their two foci, which are points near each end, which may be proved by the fact that lines drawn to them from any point on the circumference of the ellipse will exactly equal its length.

One would imagine that such a stupendous fact would be involved in a maze of incomprehensible mysteries; but no; there it is, in our simple 3 x 4 lodge floor, and the symbol of the sun is present to attest that those who put it there knew what they were about.

Form of lodge floor in true proportions of 3x4.

The repetitions of our lodge floor proportions in the floor plans of ancient temples, facing the East, so as to catch the first rays of the rising sun, the use of a 3 x 4 oblong by the ancients as a frame for representations of the sun god Helios and of Apollo, the elliptical figures of the wonderful little Egyptian scarabæus amulets, most of which, like the royal cartouches, bear the name of a Pharaoh, beginning with a symbol of the sun placed in one of the foci and the winged disk of the sun god Ra, over the portals of every Egyptian temple, all attest that these wonderful truths were known ages before the beginning of human history.

As the form of the lodge develops our conception of the orbit of our earth about the sun, so we are able to advance in understanding of other features of surpassing importance. This checkered floor pattern was not there by chance; it was in fact one of the world's earliest scientific instruments. All engineers make use of what is called the *equation of loci* in registering the rise and fall of temperature, electricity, water and steam pressure, terrestrial levels, comparative costs, etc., by zigzagging a colored line through a maze of geometrical squares. In this very manner, by the movements of the long, needlelike shadows cast upon the surface of such temple pavements by obelisks at their corners and in their centers, the sun was made to register innumerable facts concerning its relation to the earth, while the differences between the facts registered at different points taught the lessons of comparative latitudes and longitudes, the shape and size of the earth, and the conditions on different parts of its surface.

These were a few of the circumstances that caused the "oblong square, one-third longer from east to west than from north to south," indicating also the motion of all the planets, from west to east, to be regarded as a philosophical epitome of the universe.

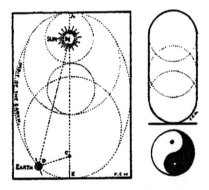

The earth's orbit as imagined by the Egyptian Astronomers. As it goes round the sun the sum of the lines B-D and D-C should always equal the length of A-E. The true ellipse is, however, far nearer a circular form which places the sun close to the centre. The upper right-hand cut shows the cartouche in which every Pharaoh's name was inscribed. The picture below it shows the sun-and-shadow figure of the ancient Chinese, derived from the figure above.

The Candidate

In all ancient rites and mysteries the participants in which were received by initiation, the greatest care was always exercised with respect to certain details, which if not properly carried out might mar or invalidate the entire ceremony.

The true significance of all initiation has ever been that of a spiritual rebirth. The sacred Agrouchada of the Hindu says, ''The first birth is merely the advent into material life; the second birth is the entrance to a spiritual life.''

The newly initiated into the first degree of Brahmanism was called *dowidja,* which means ''twice born.'' The very word *initiate* indicates that the candidate is at least symbolically in the same situation as if he had had no previous existence. He is to be ushered into an altogether new world.

In ancient initiations the extremity of humility was expressed by the rent garments of contrition for past offenses in the life about to be blotted out, the bosom offered to the executioneer's sword, and the attitude of a captive.

The most curious customs perhaps had to do with what might be termed the complete preparation of the candidate against the influences that had affected his previous career. During the multitude of centuries in the course of which astrology was thought to play the strongest part in human affairs, every circumstance affecting the welfare of humanity was deemed to have its rise in one or another of the planets, or perhaps in a lucky or evil combination of several. The science of medicine rose entirely from this curious belief in planetary affinities. The ancient physician diagnosed his patient's malady according to the diseases listed under the latter's unlucky stars and tried to cure it by application of substances designated as governed by those planets favorable to him. The same idea governed the individual with reference to articles carried upon his person. The superstitious carried various charms and amulets intended to draw favorable planetary influences to his aid, and was just as careful to avoid substances that might produce a contrary effect.

In the ordering of the candidate for initiation into the ancient mysteries this belief played an important part. The candidate might carry upon his person nothing that would invite the attention of occult planetary powers through the mysterious tie that bound them to terrestrial objects.

The lists of plants, flowers, minerals, metals, and other things that were subject to these mysterious influences were long and complicated. Gold linked him with the sun, which incited to the besetting sin of intellectual pride; silver drew upon him the fickle qualities of the Moon: copper, sacred to Venus, provoked lust, and iron, the metal of Mars, quarrelsomeness; tin, tyranny and oppression, the qualities of Jupiter; lead, sloth and indolence, belonging to Saturn; while mercury or quicksilver was responsible for dishonesty and covetousness. Therefore a key or a coin, and above all a sword, was likely to bring confusion upon the whole mysterious operation of regeneration.

Above all were enjoined upon the candidate the three sacred virtues, which by the Jain sects in India are still called "the three jewels," represented by three circles, "right belief," "right knowledge," and "right conduct." In order to reach the spiritual plane, in which the soul is entirely freed from the bonds of matter, these were the chief necessities, and the person who clung to them would certainly go higher until he reached the state of liberation.

To the ancient candidate were also recommended "the three successive steps which open the soul to free and unobstructed activity and communication on both the psychic and the spiritual planes. The first was to still the ego and empty the mind of every bias and standard of self and sense. The second consisted, when this passive state had been induced, in fixing and holding the attention upon the specific object about which the truth was desired.

Thirdly, the foregoing two steps having been taken, the individual was to stand firmly and persistently in the receptive and listening attitude for the immediate revelation of the truth, *in the full expectation of getting it*. This receptive state and expectant attitude opened the consciousness to "the psychic vibrations that write unerringly their story on the receptive mind."

Whom Does the Candidate Represent?

Within the simple and easily formulated problem asked in the heading is contained the sublimest of all secrets, which various of the higher degrees have sought to answer, each in its own way. It involves the intimate application of all the symbolic degrees *to the initiate himself,* without which they are as empty as air.

In all the ancient mysteries a character was assumed by the candidate, and as the candidates were many and the character depicted always the same, it must have represented something essentially common to all alike. Furthermore, the precise similarity of the experiences to which each individual candidate was subjected argued the identical lesson in all cases.

Examination of all available detail, especially the sacred writings of many races, confirms us in the conviction that this universal character was but an allegorical representation of the

The trial of the Dead.

Ego or "self," engaged in the warfare of which it has been said that the victor is "greater than he who taketh a city" and emerging a conqueror in the very instant of apparent defeat. We receive our earliest concrete presentation of such a character in the celebrated document known as the Egyptian Book of the Dead, the Bible of the builders of the Pyramids, fragments of which are found wrapped in the cloths of almost every mummy.

The Book of the Dead presents the wanderings of a departed soul through the underworld to the council of the gods, who were to listen to its accusers, give heed to its defenders, and finally weigh its accumulated good deeds in the scales against the feather symbol of "truth." The name of this character is given as *Ani* the Scribe. It finally transpired that this name was equivalent to the Latin term *ego,* meaning the "I Am" or "self" in man. This leads to what was perhaps the greatest and most important of all secret teachings of the ancient world, one that has become so obscured *by the confusion of its many dramatic representations with real historical characters,*—that most clear and careful labor is required to trace the main ideas from age to age and people to people, in order to show that they are fundamentally, everywhere, exactly the same.

There is no difficulty whatever in recognizing the self-conscious principle in every man as being an actual spark of the infinite self-consciousness precipitated into material existence, through the labyrinth of which it is compelled to strive in ceaseless search for the Master's Word, the secret of its being and immortal destiny. If this idea of the struggle of a divine and immortal soul, weighed down with the burden of matter and assailed at every turn by foes that symbolize the continual transformations of matter from "life" to "death" and "death" to "life," be taken as the vital principle of every drama of regeneration, from the "Book of the Dead" to John Bunyan's "Pilgrim's Progress," we too shall have progressed a long way upon the road to understanding, that of Freemasonry.

The beautiful star that is the chief emblem of the Royal Arch degree, besides being the sacred symbol of Israel, has had no other meaning during the thousands of years from the most ancient Brahmanism to the Temple of today. Even when called "the United Seal of *Vishnu* and *Siva*," the "Immortal" and the "Mortal," or "Fire" the symbol of Spirit, and "Water" the symbol of Matter, it represented the same idea, that of the "Self Conqueror," *the Perfect Man,* who had learned the subjugation of human passions and perfection in attitude toward God and fellow man. Thus the up-pointing triangle stood for *the ascent of matter into spirit* which is typified by the phrase "resurrection of the body," and the down-pointing triangle *the descent of spirit into matter,* and the complete star represents the immortal being fitted to dwell in "that house not built with hands, eternal in the heavens."

The Widow's Son

No character in history could boast of such distinguished antecedents as this remarkable personage, who has been the central figure of the spiritual world to so many generations, of so many races, stretching back into a dawn antedating the beginning of written records. To what extent his pathetic figure still dominates the souls of men must be left to the individual student to determine.

Babylonian goddess Ishtar standing on Lion, with star Spica Virginis, on head.

Our Masonic cognizance of such a figure is derived entirely from the biblical story of the planning and erection of King Solomon's Temple at Jerusalem, through friendly co-operation between the neighborly monarchs of Israel and Tyre.

Archeological science, added to an intelligent reading of Scripture, during recent years has added much to the knowledge possessed by mankind of actual conditions in those distant days. The story of the application of the King of Israel to his cousin of Tyre for technical and material assistance in the construction of a Temple to the Most High is today readily explained by the fact

Egyptian goddess Isis, as the harvest Virgin.

that many of the features embodied in the descriptions of this Temple that remain to us were common to the Temples erected by the Phenicians not only of Tyre, Sidon, Tarshish, Ashkelon, Joppa, Gaza, and other coast cities about the eastern end of the Mediterranean Sea, but also in Crete, Cyprus, Carthage, and the Punic settlements in Spain. The religious differences that separated the various Semitic peoples of Asia Minor were less fundamental than most people imagine.

Lest it be inferred that we are controverting the teaching of Holy Writ on this particular subject, attention is called to the 26th, 27th, and 28th chapters of Ezekiel, which describe the apostasy of the Tyrians from a common worship of the true God with the Israelites and their impending punishment therefor.

74

It must not be forgotten that the Great and Sacred Name was unrepeatable in all circumstances. It was the priceless sacerdotal secret, and the wisdom of the ancient seers consisted in demonstrating it to be the root of all manifested being.

The names *Baal* and *Moloch,* which, we are commonly told, were those of sanguinary Phenician gods, were simply the words "Lord" and "King," applied quite as frequently by the Jews as by the Tyrians to the common object of worship.

Isis and the Infant Horus.

The rock on which the Jews split from the other Semitic peoples was that of "graven images" and the multiplication of minor gods representing the attributes of the One, or the forces of Nature. The philosophy underlying the religious ideas of the two peoples was essentially the same. It was a "year" cult, which took cognizance of the annual journey of the earth round the sun and of the wonderful metamorphoses of Nature occurring with unerring regularity during its progress.

The character employed in the mysteries of these ancient peoples was identically the same as the smiling babe whom we represent as bowing his way in with New Year greetings on Jan. 1 and departing, a sour and forbidding old Grandfather Time, the following Dec. 31. This character was common to all Semitic peoples from the Tigris to the Mediterranean and to the Egyptians, and in fact far deeper into the East; for he came originally from India.

He was a personification of that which the Greek philosophers called the *Logos,* which meant the "Word" or "Builder," the active manifestation of Deity that is forever busy renewing the face of the earth, through its vegetable and animal life, the fertilizing and fructifying principle, operating principally through the medium of sex. The continually recurrent phenomena of the year invested this character with the attributes of a god who was a vigorous youth at the vernal equinox, rose to power and glory at the summer solstice, was set upon and slain in the autumn months, buried in the winter, rising from the dead or being reborn as an infant at the winter solstice—a perpetual round, going on forever. The ancients could conceive of no reproduction except in terms of sex, and so it was always the male principle that fertilized and the female principle that received and nursed the germs of life, bringing them forth at the appointed times, able again to reproduce the unending life transmitted through them.

In the Semitic story of the year, common to all, in closely related forms, the marriage of the male and female principles occurred annually at the awakening of vegetation and the mating season of the animal kingdom. Then Horus, the spirit of fertility, represented by the position of the sun in the zodiacal sign of the Ram, called *Ammon*, united with Virgin Nature, personified by the position of the earth in the sign of Virgo, goddess of

Alexandrian coins of the Caesars, showing Hermes on the Ram, entering the year as Harpocrates and leaving it for the underworld as Serapis. Later forms of Horus and Osiris.

the grain harvest, holding in her hand the sheaf of wheat called by the Hebrews *shibboleth,* in the midst of which glistens the brilliant star named Abib (now termed *spica Virginis*), which gave its name to the month of the Passover. The name Horus-Ammon is the same as *Khurum* and *Churam* (translated "Hiram") among the Phenicians.

In the Hebrew arrangement of the 12 sons of Jacob, as representative of the 12 signs of the zodiac, the month of the Ram falls to Reuben, which name is an acrostic of the words *Ben Aur,* or "Son of Light," which is precisely the original meaning of the name Horus. The sign of Virgo was represented by the tribe of Naphtali.

In all the old Semitic mystery dramas of the year, the Father and Son were identical. The fertile principle espoused the virgin Nature, and perished, leaving his consort a widow; but she brought forth the same fertile principle anew, as a son, who would in due time become again her husband.

The characters were called Horus and Isis in Egypt, Bel and Ishtar in Babylonia, Baal and Ashtoreth (or Astarte) in Phenicia, and are introduced into the gorgeous imagery of the building of King Solomon's Temple as the Tyrian architect whose mother was a widow of the tribe of Naphtali. The gold, silver, and brass, the fine linen, scarlet, purple, and blue, in which the celebrated artist was such an accomplished worker, did not mean the material metals and colors that they seem at first glance; they were the ancient imageries of the planetary influences and elementary substancs that served as the material bases of all manifested creation.

Isis and the infant Horus on an Alexandrian coin of the Caesars.

The Lodge Heads

Given, as our point of departure, the analogy between lodge and universe as the theater of a drama of human development, it is not difficult to take the next logical step and show the various characters of the Masonic legend to be but personifications of celestial influences.

The oldest archeological remains of both the Babylonians and the Egyptians show that the chief actors in their Mysteries were personifications of the seven planets visible to the naked eye, which are symbolized by the *menorah* or seven-branched candlestick, and the 12 animal figures that represented corresponding months of the year.

Minerva investing the two Hermes (mercury and Hercules) with the symbol of 3x3. — From a Greek vase 3,000 years old.

It has been said that the ancients never inquired what caused rain or thunder; but that their questions were "Who rains?" and "Who thunders?" and when they were answered "Jove," their curiosity was quite satisfied.

Therefore the inception of all legendary lore belongs to a time when the human was still primitive, but when, nevertheless, vague glimmerings of true science were beginning to knock for admission into his wondering mind. The very hard word *anthropomorphism* (meaning, according to learned definition, "the representation of the Deity in the form of a man, or with bodily parts: the ascription to Deity of human affections and passions") had to be invented, from the Greek words meaning "man" and "form," to describe just what we must understand when a whole assemblage of gods is presented to us as residents of some vast Olympus, Walhalla, or other heavenly domain, in which they walk and talk, love and hate, commune and quarrel, like mortals below.

The real secret of the ancient priesthoods and wise men who stood sponsors for this system was that all the varied figures of whom they discoursed so eloquently and who inspired the lyre of a Homer and the chisel of a Praxiteles were but the philosophical attributes of a single undivided, omnipotent, omnipresent Being who delighted to live, thus veiled, from His creatures. Thus the universe itself, "that in which we live and move and have our being," was the true manifestation of Deity, and every one of its many discernible parts was one of the emanations or attributes of Divinity, executing His mandates as though with separate intelligence.

In pursuance of this grand and all-embracing conception, the Mysteries confronted their candidates, successively, with all the various figures chosen, impressing them one by one, until the final revelation that they but constituted a stupendous Unity, a beautiful, perfect, and complete Whole.

Nothing more suitable or appropriate could have been chosen than the ever-recurring story of the year, from its joyful beginning to its tragic end and miraculous resuscitation by the divine hand. Every age and race during thousands of years has had its own particular version of this great annual cosmic drama, so easily recognized by the arithmetical quantities of its leading characters,—*three* for the chief characters, *seven* for the next in rank, and *twelve* for the group for which the Greeks invented the significant name of "chorus."

The great genius of Israel consisted *in taking the selfsame elements from which were constructed all the ancient paganisms* and erecting the wonderful and significant allegory of the building of King Solomon's Temple, a figure of the co-operation between God and man, in the building of the House eternal of the future, from the coarse matter of present environment and possibilities.

We can scarcely imagine what the religions of humanity must have been like before the inception of this cosmic science; for it is the wellspring and fountain of every manner and method of religious expression in all times and places of which we have any knowledge. There is no known name of Deity that is not a hidden clue to the perfection of the universe, from a geometrical or mathematical viewpoint, while the "Ministers of God," unveiled, are those great processes of generation and regeneration which are going on everywhere about us.

If the lodge, therefore, represents the universe, it also represents the ancient philosophical conception of the universe as the manifestation of God to the seer, and the officers of the lodge sit in their several stations as did the priests in the holy places of old, to exemplify and explain the mysteries of God's working through Nature, above and below.

The triple character of the principal officers of the lodge is significant in the extreme. Those who are prone to imagine that the mystery of the Trinity is a sectarian dogma have but to examine the subject more particularly to discover a triple aspect of unity in Deity that is as old as human thought and belongs to the infancy of civilization. The Jews possess it, as deeply rooted as any other people, in their cabalistic philosophy of the universe, worked out in the letters of the Hebrew alphabet, used mathematically, as *Jod, Heh,* and *Vav.* As the ancients combined astronomy with philosophy in elaborating those wonderful cosmic dramas which have focussed the human mind with reverence upon our Creator, so during many milleniums the chief ambassador of Deity to man, "the messenger of the Gods" was the spirit of the planet Mercury, closest to the sun, which, ever rising above and falling below the latter, sometimes appears as "morning" and sometimes as "evening" star, and often passes through "the lion's skin," the fiery corona of his celestial master, King Sol-Om-On.

The twins Gemini are the two last-named aspects of Mercury, the Divine Beauty and the Divine Power (or Strength), Apollo and Hercules; while the sign of Virgo, which the ancient Hebrews assigned to the tribe of Naphthali, is the astrological "day house" of Mercury, whose Greek name is *Hermes* (the Divine Wisdom), from the Egyptian *Chr-Amun,* translated by the Phenicians into *Khurum* and the Hebrews into *Hirm.* Hercules, the great God of Phenicia, was by the Tyrians called Melkarth, King of the City (of Tyre).

Therefore we at once perceive the warrant for the Hermes of Gemini, the Hermes of Virgo (the "conductor of souls"), and the Apollo who (*Dumuzi,* the *Tammuz* of the Semites, and the *Adonis* of the Greeks) was made by them to tell the story of the year and the transient character of all beauty in nature; which, notwithstanding its utter destruction during the winter months, forever revives at the call of the Master's Word.

Our Three Grand-Masters

It is quite possible for the hero of a popular legend to be at once real and unreal. The real character will be or has been the indistinct historical personage about whom, when sober sense is allowed to assert itself over sentimental enthusiasm, we must admit we know little or nothing based upon profane history or archeological remains. On the other hand, the poetry and song of an inspired race have often wrapped their national aspirations about some chance-indicated figure and produced a demigod.

Our three ancient operative Grand Masters are representative of both these two classes in an eminent degree. Of their historical proportions we are poorly informed; but of their undying fame there is ample guaranty. Upon the universal mystery hypothesis, they represent at one and the same time the powers that direct the forces of terrestrial nature and those which reign over the soul of man.

Their ritualistic associations with the three divine attributes, Wisdom, Strength, and Beauty, link them almost automatically with the three ancient names most intimately associated with these qualities,— Solomon of Israel, Melkarth the Tyrian Hercules, and Adonis the Syrian Apollo (whose name forms part of that of Adon-

"Ehoohu." the Egyptian god of the Mysteries. A Horus figure with Harvester's flail and Shepherd's Crook.

iram or Adonhiram, "the Lord Hiram"). The name *Adon* was synonymous with *Baal* or *Bel*, meaning "Lord"; the name *Melkarth* was composed in part of *Melech*, "King." If we were speaking in terms of Greek or Roman mythology, we should call these three personages simply Helios (or Sol), Hercules, and Apollo. The latter pair is the zodiacal sign of *Gemini*, the twins, who

The child Horus on an Alexandrian coin of the Caesars.

81

with the Hermes of *Virgo* constitute the threefold or Thrice-great Hermes of ancient philosophy, astronomically the planet Mercury.

These apparent individual parts were deemed by the priests to represent but attributes of the Creator; but even as such, they were the particular attributes most intimately associated with the creation and destiny of man, whose chief ornaments and distinctions from the baser creations about him were endowments of this same Wisdom, Strength, and Beauty, in which resided his likeness to his Divine Maker. Wisdom was the special solar attribute.

The life story of the Ego lends itself aptly to an allegory in which these three supreme divine gifts figure in the leading roles. The distribution of emblems to the three principal lodge officers tell a story in itself.

The three squares that are the symbols of the three ancient operative Grand Masters are three angles of 90 degrees, a total of 270, the mystery number of human existence, derived from the days of gestation.

The square, alone, is the symbol of creative wisdom, the plumb of the upright stature of the living man, and the level the recumbent posture of death, closely assimilating the three stations with the original Aryan symbolism of Brahma the Creator, Vishnu the Preserver, and Shiva the Transformer. It is significant that of these three qualities Beauty should be singled out as the eternally perishing and eternally reviving quality of the manifested universe. The modern scientist tells us that all matter consists of vortices of positive and negative electrons, revolving round each other with incredible speed, the emanations of the Infinite Mind arranging themselves into harmonious forms, determined by the same Infinite Mind.

Here is the analogy in a nutshell: The determining Wisdom is always there, the Infinite Power is always present; the form alone is perishable and displays the alternate phenomena that we call "birth" and "death," although the essence is deathless. This is the true significance of the mystery deaths of all of the beautiful nature-gods such as Osiris, Dumuzi, Tammuz, Dionysus, Adonis, Atys, a host of diverse racial names, but one and the same representation of the same cosmic fact,—that the sole thing of all creation that perishes or "dies" as we misunderstand death, is the quality of form, perceptible to the material senses.

It is this one of our three Grand Masters that displays the pattern upon the trestle-board from which, once executed, it will be erased to make way for another. It is this one that is symbolized by the sun poised but an instant at the meridian ere its descent to the portals of the west begins. It is this one that, with finger pressed on lip, guards with his very existence the secret of his art until the capstone of the edifice he is charged to erect-shall be placed in position and the whole work dedicated to its glorious ultimate purpose in the counsel of the Most High.

Truly, at the approach of winter storms and icy blasts, the trestleboard of Nature's Temple is void of directions for the workman and the plans of Divine Wisdom and Power inoperative in the absence of the *manifesting* syllable of the creative word! There is but one substitute in the ordering of matter from chaos to form; for the handiwork of the Great Architect himself and the secret lies in the triple square of the Supreme Three,—"Man."

The mystery of human life.

The Twelve Fellowcrafts

Man is unable to comprehend eternity in any other sense than that of a circle. The greatest god of all the old pantheons always represented Time, and he was the father of all the other gods. He carried in his hand a straight line and a circle. The first had beginning and end, the second neither. This represented Time and Eternity. The straight line divided into 12 equal parts also represented Matter. From it was constructed the greater cosmic triangle of 3, 4, and 5 parts, the foundation of all geometrical science.

The solar universe, constituting a stupendous clock, keeping more perfect time, in the divinely adjusted revolutions of all its parts, than the most perfect chronometer of human workmanship, naturally conveys the notion of periodic time and also furnishes the means for its measurement, in the circular courses of the planets round the great dial of the ecliptic. The almost circular but still elliptical course of the earth round the sun supplies the means of measuring the course of the year, with its series of identical, ever-recurring phenomena, upon which the whole course of human life is based.

The division of this year-circle into 12 equal parts is one of the pillars of geometry, as its further section into 360 is of mathematics. Neither is an arbitrary process, but each is founded on fixed natural principles.

The allegory of King Solomon's Temple so closely parallel, upon real historical happenings to a material edifice, was that of the fruitful year, with its bountiful harvest and various other blessings, scarcely erected and dedicated ere falling into destruction and decay.

The story of the annual building of the Temple, its destruction and restoration in three days, the untimely loss of its chief architect and of his miraculous revival for the purpose of continuing his labors, is the theme of legends as old as the Pyramids, if not older, and has been told in many different ways to various races and ages.

Strange to say, they do not transpire in the biblical account of the building of King Solomon's Temple. Our first trace of them is away back in old Babylonia where a mystery drama was performed by the priests, showing the adventures of a mythical hero, sometimes called Gilgamesh and sometimes Izdubar, who was slain and revived at the winter solstice. This was when the winter solstice was in Pisces, and so the hierophants were dressed as fish and were surrounded by 10 other figures wearing animal heads as masks representatives of the months. The hero was of course the month of the Ram, making 12 in all. The story of Joseph and his brethren is a beautiful rendition of this universal mystery drama.

The Hebrews never discarded the profound scientific knowledge of their Chaldean ancestors, but diverted it from the idolatrous misuses into which it had fallen, doing away with the idea of gods as month representatives for that of patriarchs, worshipers of the one true God of Israel.

The whole scheme was undoubtedly what we should now call astrological. Men were supposed to derive their qualities from the celestial powers, as indicated by the relative positions of the planets at the time they were born, and indeed the world only generally discarded this notion a few hundred years since, while many still find it a serious contemplation.

When Joshua led the victorious Israelites across the Jordan, upon their entrance into the promised land he selected a representative of each tribe as the bearer of a stone, afterward erected as a memorial at a place called "Gilgal." This name is the term now given by savants to all such stone circles found throughout the Orient, and as they are frequent it shows that a ceremonial in honor of the year was common in the East and that the ritualistic stations were 12 in number, hierophants representing the sun, moon, and planets performing what we should term the "floor work."

These ceremonies spread to the West, and were the basis of Druidism. The 12-stone circles remain in many parts of Europe. The stories of Samson and Hercules are founded on them.

Elijah erected one of these circles, in the midst of which he placed his sun altar when he confuted the priests of Baal.

We find the number 12 predominating in all the arrangements of the Israelites. Twelve oxen supported the great laver in King Solomon's Temple, and 12 lions led to his throne. The selection of 12 apostles was in obedience to this most ancient of traditions.

There were *three other* fellowcrafts associated with the age-old mystery play; but they were not month signs; they were the three winter planets, Mars, Jupiter, and Saturn. The twelve worthy brethren really got along very well in life because the Greeks and Romans were so well pleased with their performances that they promoted them to be the gods of Olympus.

The twelve gods of Olympus identified as the signs of the Zodiac, on a Roman altar.

The Cable Tow

Numerous monuments of antiquity attest the long-established usage of leading captives before their conquerors or judges by means of cords attached to various parts of the body. This was a mark of degradation for the victim and contributed  to the exultation of the victor. Assyrian, Babylonian, Egyptian, and other sculptures of great age exhibit long defiles of prisoners, led in triumph by cords about their necks or even passed through their nostrils; while ancient Mexican monuments show that the tongues of prisoners were frequently slit to receive a cord by which they were haled before the monarch.

The Serpent Wand of Hermes.

In medieval paintings of the "Stations of the Cross," which represent the various episodes in the final scene of the Gospels, particular stress seems to be laid upon the cord by which Jesus is led to execution —and a curious but persistent difference is often found in connection with His three falls on the way to Calvary. He starts from the audience hall of the Roman governor, Pilate, led by a cord passed round his neck. Then this cord seemingly wanders to his arm or wrist, and in the final scenes it is invariably round his waist. This may or may not be significant; but it is always so portrayed.

Our minds, however, are led from the purely utilitarian employment of cords, for the purpose of preventing escape, to their ceremonial significance, when the victim was not a prisoner whom it was sought to degrade, but an animal or a captive to be sacrificed as a popular offering to the gods, in which case the cord might be of silk and was often entwined with a garland of flowers.

The assumption of cords as girdles, halters, and other emblems of voluntary submission was always expected of citizens surrendering the keys of their conquered city and practised by members of religious orders in token of humility and subjection to the heads of their confraternities. This latter custom is as common among the Buddhists of Ch-2 Asia as among the Roman monks of the Western World.

The cord as a completely ceremonial symbol is one of the oldest known, and was the particular badge of the initiate into the mysteries of the Brahmins. The manufacture of such cords, with reference to the number and color of threads entering into their composition, was the subject of sacred detail, to come directly to the fact that a thrice-turned cable tow or cord of three loops was one of the best known of ancient Hermetic emblems.

"Ch-R,"
Horus.

In the Egyptian hieroglyphic system it was the equivalent to the Hebrew letter *Cheth* or *Ch*, having a numerical value of 8, and the initial of the Egyptian sacred name commonly known, from its Greek rendition, as *Horus*. Every such name, however, was composed of cabalistic elements known to the priests alone. The complete name was simply the two letters *Cheth* and *Resh* (*Chr*), of which the monogram X-P, much employed in Christian art, in which it is wrongfully called *Chi-Rho*, was the symbol many centuries B. C.

Briefly, the word *Chr* is a transposition of the Sanscrit *Rch* meaning "light." The ancient sacred writings of the East reveal the fact that light was considered the original primordial material; so that when God said "Let there be light" He was not merely illuminating that which had already been created, but this was, in fact, the first creative act of the Great Architect.

The letter *Rho* or R represented the value of 100, the square on the hypotenuse of a right angle of 36-64, the particular figure of the 47th problem, that, to the Egyptians, suggested spirit, matter, and spirit and matter combined, which latter, the child of the first two, was *Horus,* or the fertile principle of Nature. Astronomically, *Ch* was the letter of *Amun* the lamb, the zodiacal sign of *Aries,* the beginning of spring; *R*, the planet Mercury, or *Chr-Mse,* the "Son or Horus." The combination was Horus-Amun, or the *Hirm* of the Hebrews and the names of the month of the Lamb or Ram (among the Jews, *Abib*), now called *Nisan,* from the Chaldean *Nisannu.*

Christian
Symbol of
Redeemer

Mathematically, the sum of the first eight digits was 36, the number of the Sun, which was further developed by adding the numbers 1 to 36, giving 666, which revealed the sun (*Shin-Mem-Shin, Shamash,* equaling 640) as the physical vesture of J H V H (26).

The Egyptians, circumscribing the oblong of 3 x 4 with a perfect circle, found the latter divided into segments of 72, 108, 72, 108 degrees. Such saucer-shaped segments were among their most sacred symbols, and represented the word *Neb* or "Lord," equivalent to the Phenician *Baal.* The triple-looped character *Ch,* passing through the lozenge-shaped *R* (Vescica Piscis), represented the perpetual reincarnation of life by passage through the womb of Nature. Ancient Hindu astrology had placed the extreme limit of human life at 108 years; so that twice 108, or 216, was the philosophical number of "rebirth" or reincarnation. This number was produced by grouping the first eight digits in this manner:

$$\begin{array}{cc} 4 & 5 \\ 6 & 3 \\ 2 & 7 \\ 8 & 1 \\ \hline \multicolumn{2}{c}{216} \end{array}$$

A tracing through the number in numerical sequence will show the meaning of this triple loop; which is, by the way, only one of a wide variety of combinations of these eight numbers upon which the cabalistic philosophy of all ancient peoples, including the Chinese, are based. It will be noticed that all such numbers are multiples of nine or "3 times 3," the significance of which cannot escape notice. The two serpents entwined round the caduceus, or wand of Hermes, represent this figure, as the three three-petaled almond flowers of Aaron's rod on the shekels of Israel allude to the same philosophy, which is the unchanging basis of all Freemasonry and its symbolism.

Therefore, if we are to find any significance in the cable tow derived from the thrice-looped cord of Hermes, it is the bond uniting spirit to matter, or soul to body, by which our divine part is held captive by our mortal constituents until "the golden bowl is broken and the silken cord is loosened."

Angles

Among the great variety of architectural allusions abounding in Masonic parlance, those relating to ''angles'' receive relatively little attention, whereas they constitute very important clues to the significance of the whole system.

We have advanced far enough in our investigations to have perceived that the underlying principle of all mysteries of philosophy and religion, past and present, have been what might be termed ''ciphers'' or ''cryptograms'' of the ascertained phenomena of nature; in fact, science, almost smothered in superstition, struggling to attain individual expression as the truth that should set men free.

There are nevertheless wonders in Freemasonry, inherited from the Ancient Mysteries, for which there are no purely human explanations, because they are manifested upon an infinite scale. Geometry is the key, and close observation of the angles of certain squares and oblongs shows it to be the medium through which we may hope to obtain a little more light upon this fascinating subject.

Wherever two lines, traveling in whatsoever directions, cross each other, the point at which they cross may be the center of a circle of any desired extent, divided into 360 degrees, the number of which, separating the two lines as they cross the circle, is the correct *angle* described by such lines.

There are therefore two ways of expressing any plane surface so that another may reproduce it from the description. One is to give its length and breadth. The other is to give its angles.

The most important angle in geometry is one of 90 degrees, or the fourth part of a circle. The upright is determined by the force we call ''gravity,'' causing the bob of the *plumb* to point directly to the center of the earth. The horizontal line is determined by the bubble of air in the center of our *level* seeking. an exact equilibrium for its resting point. When we shall have truly adjusted both plumb and level, our reward will be the definition of a perfect *square* or angle of 90 degrees, with reference to the great circle of the heavens.

This angle will be still further accentuated in our minds, when we perceive the Sun, at meridian, precisely over our heads and realize that a line from the Sun to the point at which we stand and thence deflected to the horizon, would be this same angle of 90 degrees.

It will be discovered that some of the most important features of God's creation are inextricably built round the precise geometrical relation of a square to a circle, and that this fact appears prominently in the Masonic ritual.

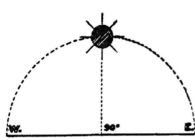

The Sun at Meridian.

As we advance in the knowledge of physical laws, especially in the domain of mechanics, we cannot fail to perceive the dependence of every minor consideration upon the great, all-embracing cosmic necessity defined by *plumb*, *level*, and *square*.

The ancient seer, however, having divined the eternal fixity and cosmic character of the right angle of 90 degrees, sought deeper truths in the many natural combinations of right angles with those of other degrees, in the elaboration of the simplest and most useful in calculation of all plane surfaces,—triangles.

The cosmic wonder in this particular figure is the celebrated Triangle of Pythagoras, allusions to which have been continually cropping up in the course of these papers and from which we shall never quite depart.

Neglecting for the moment its association with the great problem of Euclid, of which it is the basis, we find it to be the product of the diagonal division of an oblong of 3x4, the same that gives us the form of our lodge. The angle of this oblong is one of 37 degrees.

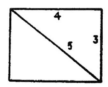

We shall now perform the operation known as the (Pythagorean) "trisection of an oblong," which consists in making a second and shorter diagonal, from the lower left-hand corner of the oblong in question, joining at right angles with the first. The joining of these two inner lines, with the heel of the left in the hollow of the right line, divides the oblong into three parts of precisely identical form, but nicely graduated proportions, each of which is as 3 to 4 and 5, and all of which respond to the following magic square:

There is no doubt about the application we are about to suggest; for we find it on early Bactrian coins of about 120 B. C. in conjunction with the zodiacal figures of the spring equinox and summer solstice, the Lion and Bull, and the ancient Hindu symbol of light, *Rch* (X-P).

$$\begin{array}{ccc} 9 & 12 & 15 \\ 12 & 16 & 20 \\ 15 & 20 & 25 \\ \hline 36 & 48 & 60 \end{array}$$

The sum total of the square is 144, the square of 12, which was expressed by the breastplate of the Jewish high priest; but the multiplication together of 36, 48, and 60 gives 103,680, or four times 25,920, the duration, in years, of a complete precession of the equinoxes. One of the greatest of the ancient conceptions of Deity was as "Boundless Time," in which He was represented by the slow-moving planet Saturn or *Cronos*, whom we best know today as "Father Time," of the scythe and hour-glass. Saturn was *BRAMA* among the Hindus, and *ABRAM* among the Semites. The numerical value of these letters is A 1, B 2, R 100, A 1, M 40, or 144, which exactly corresponds to the Th 9, E 5, O 70, S 60, *ThEOS* of the Greeks, from which we get our word "Theology," etc. The student will not fail to discover, in the figures given, the great influence of Euclid's famous 47th problem; for 9, 16, and 25 are the squares of 3, 4, and 5, of which it is constructed.

Bactrian coin of King Azes, B. C. 120.

Signs

Students on the alert for signs of Masonic import in the relics of bygone ages will find them in many unexpected corners, if they know what they are and how to recognize them.

The artistic and architectural canons of the ancient world were all based upon systems of geometrical squares like those of a chessboard and the figure we have already discussed in connection with the lodge floor. An alternately colored and white paved work long ago acquired the name of "Mosaic pavement," associating it with the great Hebrew seer and lawgiver, and particularly with the tradition of such a pavement having been the "pattern" exhibited upon the holy mount and alluded to in Exodus xxiv, 10, "And they saw the God of Israel; and the place under his feet was *like a paved work,* of brilliant sapphire, and like the color of heaven in clearness." There are two eminently Masonic allusions in this verse, one to the pavement, and the other to the *blue* color, which has always been symbolic of the Hermetic philosophy; whence our "Blue" lodge, for instance.

As we might well be astonished at the frequent Biblical references to Deity in language that might be applied to a gigantic man, we must seek an explanation for them in the well authenticated philosophy of the ancients, to the effect that the Universe really was the great first-created man, who, being the pattern established by God and termed the *Macrocosmos* or "great harmony," was reproduced in multitude of the *microcosmos* or "lesser harmony." Every fiber of the being of each individual comprised in the latter class was an emanation or duplication in miniature of the stupendous original model. The language of Freemasonry cleverly conceals these ancient conceptions, because ancient initiation revealed them in detail. The whole philosophy of the "Word" (the Greek term for which is *Logos*) turns upon the organization of these harmonies from the original chaos in which "the earth was without form and void."

We have thus a poetic imagery of the manifesting Deity exhibiting to the 70 elders, convoked for the purpose, the mechanical basis of this "harmony," something wherewith and whereon

93

to reason out and apply, in imitation of Divine handiwork, to constructing monuments of human genius.

This inference is more than heightened by the following language of Exodus xxvi, 40, where, after having been given complete directions for the Tabernacle and its contents, they were admonished. "And look that thou make them after their pattern which thou wast shewn on the mount." To the undirected eye no other elements can be found in this expanse of square plane surfaces than the horizontal and perpendicular lines of their composition, joined at right angles as they cross one another.

Geometers all know, however, that by these networks of squares might be demonstrated nearly all the known harmonies of Nature; for, while every intersection of a horizontal with a perpendicular line is a center upon which the immovable leg of the compasses may be placed, any such center will be a point within a series of circles circumscribing the similar centers at any selected distance round it, while lines drawn from the center so chosen to the points on the circumference where the circle crosses the intersecting line will divide such a circle into segments, which are exact equal divisions, on the age-old scale of 360 degrees.

The Mosaic Pavement. Ancestor of the Chessboard.

All this sounds very technical; but there is really no other way of describing something that will prove simple to the student sufficiently interested to experiment with it.

The result of adhering to this process is to procure exact scales of numbers, which are termed by scientists "cosmic quantities" because they are found to be the exact numbers present in the various phenomena of Nature that may be described in mathematical or geometrical terms.

Every number connected with our measurements of time is a "cosmic number," beginning with the 7 of our weekdays, the 12 of our months, the 24 of our hours, the 52 of our weeks, the 60 of our minutes and seconds, the 28 days of our lunar month, the 30 days of our mean solar month, the 365 days 6 hours of our solar year, and above all the 72 years, 2,160 years, and 25,920 years during which the solstices and equinoxes travel backward through a degree, a sign, and the whole circle of the ecliptic respectively. The subdivision of the ecliptic from 12 signs into 36 "decans" is another cosmic number, the 270 days of human gestation another. The precise intervals of the revolutions of the principal planets round the sun give rise to others.

In fact, so precise and corresponding are these numbers (which we are constantly obliged to repeat when we are telling the story of the heavenly mechanism) with the numbers produced on these mazes of right-angled, horizontal, and perpendicular lines, that the dimensions and proportions of all the old Temples, dedicated to the glory of the Great Architect of the Universe, from the earliest pyramids to the cathedrals of Europe, are but exemplifications of this remarkable fact. We may go still further and show embodied in this remarkable system the several squarings of the circle, the visual demonstration of the squares, cubes, and roots employed in higher mathematics, all of which enter into the great harmonies of the universe and translate some strange energy into what we know as "heat," "light," "sound," "force," and mark off the periods that chop eternity into what our senses know as "time."

There are no discords in Nature. All creation is indescribable in other terms than those of square and compass.

Many books have been written to prove that the Great Pyramid was built according to minute and learned calculations, showing all the principal facts about our earth and solar system; yet the most simple analysis of this stupendous monument shows that the perpendicular axis of 10 parts, at right angles with a horizontal 16, the mathematical formula of which is 10, 5+6 +5, or *Jod-Heh-Vau-Heh,* is all there is in the world necessary to repeat the cosmic wonders of the Great Pyramid.

The Prophet Isaiah tells us (xix, 19-20), "On that day there shall be an altar to JHVH in the midst of the land of Egypt and a pillar at its border to JHVH; and it shall be for a *sign* and a testimony unto God-JHVH in the land of Egypt." Isaiah was a *real* Mason.

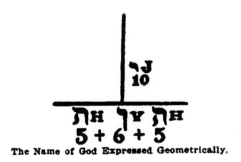

The Name of God Expressed Geometrically.

Circumambulation

The Masonic rite of circumambulation has been frequently and learnedly discussed in connection with its close resemblance to similar observances recorded as having existed among the Druids, the processionals of the priests of ancient religions, and those still practised in the Catholic, Greek, and Anglican Churches of the present day. The importance attached to ceremonial processions round land that it was intended to consecrate to some sacred employment, about edifices to be dedicated or cities to be destroyed, is amply set forth in Holy Writ and classical lore.

As a wall or hedge might surround or inclose something set apart for special reasons, so the mysticism of our forefathers imagined it possible to erect unseen spiritual barriers round objects or persons, which, according to the character of the accompanying incantations, would confine or exclude the powers of Light or Darkness as desired.

The pantheons of nearly all ancient peoples were personifications of the celestial bodies and of the constellations that served to mark the zodiacal signs and other divisions. Elaborate spectacles were therefore devised to mystify the "profane" and edify the initiates, which exhibited the movements of the sun, moon and planets among the fixed stars, especially accentuating their positions at important periods. The Sun was ever deity and king, while the hero and martyr of the various mysteries seems to have been the planet Mercury.

This latter has a triple aspect, made much use of. Situated the nearest of all our solar system to the sun, Mercury is ever to be found in the same part of the heavens. It has a year of 88 days. ("Year" in Latin, *annus,* means "a ring," or complete circle of the sun.) Part of the year Mercury rises simultaneously with the sun, when it is seen as a "morning star" for a few moments at daybreak. At another season it is seen for only a few minutes at evening, as the sun sets. Always disappearing in the intensifying solar rays, this phenomenon was likened to draping in the Lion's skin.

This star was always the character of the candidate for initiation, because Mercury was the tutelary planet presiding over the destinies of man, and its three aspects (beauty, strength, and wisdom) were the attributes of the soul, mind, and intellect.

Mercury's circumambulations of the zodiac in one solar year are four; but they are symbolically limited to three, because, while this planet "rises above" and "falls below" the sun with each of its revolutions, as a mythological personage three of these falls are characterized as due to the attack of an enemy, while the fourth, occurring close to the winter solstice, was accounted a burial, the subsequent rise from which was a resurrection. A grave error has possessed many commentators on the ancient mysteries in taking the figure of the slain hero (Adonis, Tammuz, Dionysus, etc.) to be the sun. The sun was the Supreme Being to all the ancient peoples, who, though he veiled his face in anger with storms, and removed himself afar in winter, never either died naturally or was slain. The proximity of Mercury to the sun carries that planet wherever the sun goes; hence the frequent confusion. Old Babylonian cylinder seals frequently show this final fall of Mercury between the pillars of the west with the sun-god stretching forth his hand to resuscitate him, while personifications of the three planets Saturn, Jupiter, and Mars look on accompanied by their respective attributes of water, air, and fire.

There was, however, another and equally important meaning to the circumambulations of the candidate round the imaginary circle of the heavens, and that resided in the numbers involved—108, the span of human life, was both the number and the name of Mercury (ChR); 216, or double that number, was called by the Pythagoreans the number of *metempsychosis* or reincarnation, which doctrine was once universally taught. The "thrice born" had advanced in wisdom and sanctity to the rank of a "Holy One," a fact that the Hebrews have preserved in their word *kadosh* (KDSh), which has the value of three times 108, or 324. The Hindu mystery of the 10 *avatars*, or successive births of Vishnu, illustrates the progress of the human being through successive terrestrial lives from a fish to a god. In the ninth avatar the ever-upward pursuing soul becomes a *Buddha*, completely possessed of the divine wisdom; hence nine times 108, which is the same as three times 324, or three times *Kadosh* ("Holy, Holy, Holy"); while *three times round the circle of* 360 *degrees* gives us the number 1,080, or 10 times 108, which accomplishes the rounds of rebirth in the *Kalki Avatar*, the conqueror on the white horse, with the blazing sword, whose mission it is permanently to establish righteousness and truth upon the earth.

A very few years before our era the Bactrians, whose priests were the Magi, struck coins to a historically unknown king. One side represents Apollo, capped with a rising sun, while on the other a figure seated upon a horse holds forth a cross, the surrounding inscription of which is *Soter Megas Basileus Basileon.* ("The great Savior, King of Kings"). This, with a side glance at Revelation xix, 11-16, leads us closer than ever to a perception of the great cosmic mystery involved in our Masonic journeyings in search of light.

The Origin of the Sabbath

The second section of our F.C. degree has a reference to the origin of the Jewish Sabbath, as well as the manner in which it was kept by our ancient brethren, which altogether escapes notice except as a passing Biblical reference. The fact is that it is one of the most important of the ancient cabalistic secrets of the Magian brotherhood all over the world.

Six thousand years ago the oriental mystics were satisfied among themselves that they had fathomed the complete riddle of the universe in the interesting mathematical and geometrical system that, among other things, has bequeathed the symbolism of Masonry to us. The chief secrets of the ancient ceremonies of initiation were connected with the science of astronomy.

Holy Writ tells us that "in six days God created the heavens and the earth and all that in them is." Involved in the ancient idea, however, were many circumstances well known to the seers of old, which have become lost in the lapse of ages. From the very earliest period down to the present time each one of these days has borne the name of one of the seven planets known to the ancients, and always that of the same planet to the same day, no matter how often the name of the latter has been translated from one tongue to another.

In the Biblical order of creation, God created the light on the first day, which is that of the sun.

On the second day he caused "the expansion dividing the waters," which really refers to the influence of the moon upon the tides as well as that of the sun in evaporation.

The third day vegetation came forth, which was anciently connected with the planet Mars, in the sign of the Ram, which is what so closely associated the figure of a lamb with the beginning of spring and the rebirth of vegetation after the winter's sleep.

On the fourth day, or that of Mercury, God said, "Let there be lights in the expansion of the heavens, to divide between the day and the night, and let them be for signs and seasons, days and years." This made Mercury, who was Nebo and Hermes, the patron of all the ancient arts and sciences, and thus it was that the Chaldean order of the planets (Saturn, Saturday; Jupi-

99

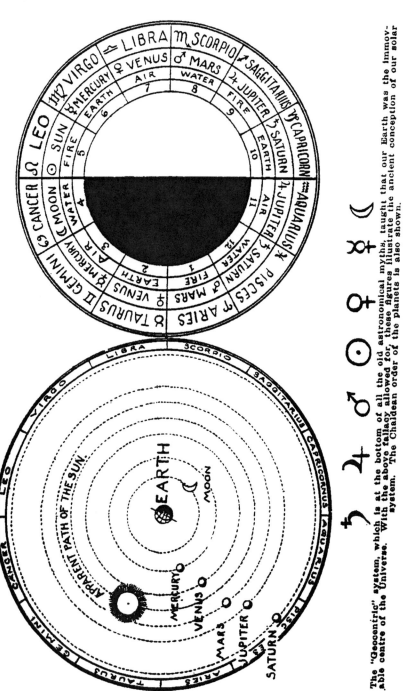

The "Geocentric" system, which is at the bottom of all the old astronomical myths, taught that our Earth was the Immovable centre of the Universe. With the above fallacy allowed for, these figures illustrate the ancient conception of our solar system. The Chaldean order of the planets is also shown.

ter, Thursday; Mars, Tuesday; Sun, Sunday; Venus, Friday; Mercury, Wednesday; Moon, Monday) was converted into the septenary division of the calendar week and an astrological system introduced which gave to the *first hour of each day* the influence of its planetary namesake, followed by that of the next on the list, until the seven had been used up. Then the list began again, with the planet of the first hour as that of the eighth, 15th, and 22d hours, and so on, in succession through the entire 168 hours of the seven-day week.

The first day of creation was naturally that which we now call "Sunday." One has only to run the Chaldean planetary order through the 24 hours of each day, beginning with the sun, in the first hour of Sunday, to discover that the correct planet begins each day.

A ready explanation for the total cessation of the Semitic world from all labor *on the day of Saturn* would be found by astrologers in the malefic astrological aspect of that planet, as the author of all evil and misfortune, of pain, sickness, and disaster, upon whose appointed day the benign creative influences desisted from all exertion and which should be employed most usefully in supplicating the Creator to avert the miseries entailed upon mankind by this most unpropitious of planets.

There is a curious and entirely physical reason to be given for the fact that the three planets, Saturn, Jupiter, and Mars, constituted the great creative trinity of Brama, Vishnu, and Siva among the Hindus in the far East, but the powers of evil throughout the western world. Students of astrology will remark the fact that they are the rulers of the whole six astrological houses (signs of the Zodiac) from Scorpio to Aries, therefore governing the winter season.

This is very different above the equator from that below, and so we must expect conceptions of its ruling planets widely different in the north from the tropics, and especially through the ages when the depth of winter lay in Pisces, a "house" of Saturn. So, when these three planets were first encountered, as the rulers of the three final winter months, which slew the fertility of the year, they were deemed three assassins or "ruffians," with, as terminations to their names, the old Aryan symbols of Brahma, Siva, and Vishnu,—A, U (or O), and M.

The Letter "G"

Many commentators on the antiquities of the craft say that the letter G that occupies the center of our distinctive emblem is merely a substitute for the Hebrew letter *Jod*, which, as the initial and representative of the ineffable name Jehovah, properly belongs there, but is replaced by G because the latter "is English." It is also often stated that our own revered Deity name "God" is simply this letter *Jod* spelled with a G.

These statements in question are only surmises, not facts. The letter G is right, and it is just where it belongs, because the true Masonic cipher is the number 3 which is a *gimel* in Hebrew and *gamma* in Greek.

Ancient philosophy always viewed the Great Architect in three aspects as Creator, Preserver, and Transformer. Nothing, said they, was ever lost. Spirit and matter were coexistent and coeternal. Matter was continually going in and out of perception, perishing apparently in one form, only to be worked over into new forms in the vast laboratory of Nature. Everything in and about the lodge is in threes, expressive of the permanence and power of this great number. The *three* side of the Pythagorean triangle represented Osiris, the male or creative principle to the Egyptians; but, though the female principle was a *four* and the offspring a *five,* and these were *three,* even if you added 3, 4, and 5 together to make 12, for 1 plus 2 made *three.* This was the way the Pythagoreans reasoned, claiming, perhaps truly, that if we understood "number" we should understand everything in creation, because all nature was but a vast arithmetical process, made visible in harmonious forms determined according to number.

Pythagoras reduced all manifestation of form to squares, circles, and triangles. The Greek letter G (*gamma*) is in the form of a Mason's square. The letter O is a circle, and the letter D (*delta*) a triangle, giving us the word "God."

These are the numbers 3, 6, and 4 alined; added together, a total of 13, but as 364 (13 times 28), the months of a lunar year, which was the origin of our 52 weeks of seven days each, adopted

Square, Circle, Triangle.

so that each day might be named for one of the seven known planets. All of the Hebrew deity names founded on the Ineffable Name were numerical multiples of 13. People were taught that this was an "unlucky" number, to keep them from investigating it.

Among the signs of the Zodiac, Gemini was the third sign, Cancer the fourth, and Virgo the sixth. In ancient Egyptian sculptures we often find representations of these three signs. Horus representing Gemini stretched upon a bier in mummy wrappings, and about to be raised to life by Isis (Virgo) standing at his head, and Nepthys (Cancer, the moon goddess) standing at his feet, the whole an allegory of the alternate perishing and reviving of Nature.

While a great many of the Semitic deity names have been accounted for as cabalistic expressions of the divine power, manifested in the continual metamorphoses of Nature, the successive returns of the seasons and the variety of scenes they display to the discerning eye, the great and sacred word, reverence to which is so deeply inculcated by Masonry, has no such historical record of its source or origin, like the word "Jehovah" communicated to Moses from the burning bush.

Philology teaches us, however, that the word "God" is an old Turanian or Scythian word for "year," still surviving with its original meaning in the Slavonic *Goda,* a year.

The ancients had several computations of calendar years at various periods, so that the analogy between 364 and a name made of these number letters, was according to the same philosophy, which turned 365 days 6 hours into JHVH by dividing each digit through the 30 degrees of the month.

Here is the manner in which the wonderful word, of such potent meaning to millions of human souls, has been entrusted to symbolism; so that so long as the symbols endure the Name committed to the adoration of the descendants of the great Indo-Germanic peoples shall not be lost.

The signs of the Zodiac, which astrology calls the "day houses of the planets," enumerated from left to right, are as follows, so placed by the Chaldeans 3,000 years before the time of Abraham: Aquarius, Pisces, Aries, Taurus, Gemini, Cancer, and Leo. The planets attributed to these houses, in sequence, are Jupiter, Saturn, Mars, Venus, Mercury, Moon, Sun, which give their names to Thursday, Saturday, Tuesday, Friday, Wednesday, Monday, Sunday, the numbers of which, as days of the week, in order given, are 5, 7, 3, 6, 4, 2, 1.

A cube or square block,—wood, stone, or other material,—geometrically regarded, has six sides. If we consider two such and add the numbers of the sides of the first, 1, 2, 3, 4, 5, 6, their total is 21. Adding the sides of the second (7, 8, 9, 10, 11, 12), the total is 57.

57—364—21

So our sequence of numbers will convey the idea of two cubes, one at the right and one at the left, with, suspended between them, the number 364, in Hebrew letters GOD.

If we push the idea a little further,—and it certainly has a far greater extension than here given,—the two numbers 21 and 57 added together amount to 78, which is three times 26, or three times JHVH, which the ancient Hebrews made to express the phrase *He that was, He that is, and He who ever shall be.*

The secret of the two Cubes.

The East

No single term associated with the hidden mysteries of ancient Freemasonry is so fraught with significance as this one "cardinal point" of the terrestrial compass. If we had no other means of surmising the common origin and purport of the world's philosophical and religious mysteries, we should still be driven to associate them with the worship of "Light" and the solar source of light by the universal orientation of temples and other sacred edifices, from the most archaic of Druidical stone heaps to the cathedrals of our own day, to the direction in which the sun daily presents its rising glory to mankind. No matter when or where, the story is always the same, and when we come to understand it rightly the reasons stand forth in a widespread ancient knowledge of many of the intimate details of Nature's inner workings.

That the sun rising in the east, to be the glory and beauty of the day, was one of the principal reasons for so placing sacred edifices that the first beams of the King of Day would enter into his holy house amid Earth's rejoicing, there can be no gainsaying; but it is equally true that this consideration is far from completely covering the question.

The two Latin words, *Oriens*, the East, and *Occidens*, the West, seem to have been derived from roots signifying the "Path of Gold" and the "Dying" or "Killing." The first is poetic, and apparently easily understandable; while the second refers to the several phenomena of nightfall and midwinter, which are always associated with the sun sinking in the West.

The organizers of the Mysteries did not leave things to chance. However vague some of their speculations might have sounded in the ears of the people, they were themselves dealing in as exact science as they were able to command. Hence, while the terrestrial "East" was ever in the direction of the rising sun, a direction that describes a complete circle with every recurring twelvemonth, the celestial or true East was permanently situated in the sign of the zodiacal lion, or *Leo*, the "House of the Sun." In every part of the world we always find the four cardinal points associated with the four elements,—East, Lion, *fire;* South, Eagle (*scorpio,*) *water;* West, man, *air;* North, Bull, *earth.**

*See Frontispiece.

We must therefore, if we are seeking to know the true significance of Masonic directions or points of the compass, look not to our perpetually moving earth, but to the relatively immovable ecliptic or circular path, round which terra firma wends its way, past the 12 way-stations (months) on its beaten track, each 30 degrees in extent and defined by a constellation of fixed stars, figuring one of the supposed animal signs of the Zodiac.

We must conceive of the universe as a whole, a gigantic being of mind, parts, and functions, so analogous to our own that we can perceive what is meant by man's being "created in God's own image." All this, to the ancients, was the manifestation of an ultimate and unmanifested power. The animating force of this vast harmony was the Sun, distributing its creative and energizing impulses by means of radiant light, and as this light carried with it the intelligence requisite to the due performance of its varied tasks, an active intelligence was deemed to reside within the luminous solar envelop, which (the manifestation, *Word,* or *Logos* of the unmanifested God) created and sustained the world and all living organisms. This *Word* was the great and sacred four-lettered word of the Hebrews, JHVH.

It can be proved by countless circumstances that JHVH was the secret God of the *whole ancient world;* only the Hebrews divested Him of the idolatrous, and often licentious and obscene rites with which He was hailed by many pagan nations. The famous number-letter philosophies of the ancient world were means by which JHVH was shown to be the source of every human science and contemplation. As the planets shone with light borrowed from the central sun, so they were, as subordinate gods, spirits or archangels, but the distributors for the central intelligence, whom the Chaldean Magi called IAO, the *Heptaktis,* or seven-rayed god. The true name of Deity was not a word simply, but a *number,* pronounced as a word, JHVH, or $10+5+6+5$, or "26," *Jehovah.* The four cardinal signs being the second, fifth, eighth, and eleventh, $2+5+8+11$ equaling 26, so these four signs represent the revealed word of God, in Christian symbology, as the symbols of the four Evangelists, taken from the visions of Ezekiel and Daniel. Relics of these four cardinal-point symbolisms, which really mean *Jehovah,* which were the true meaning of the Winged Bulls and Lions of the Assyrian temples and palaces, are scattered throughout the ruins of antiquity. There are twelve zodiacal signs of 30 degrees each, in all.

The Wise Men of the East, computing the precise length of the solar year of 365 days, 6 hours, centuries before Sosigenes, the Babylonian Jew, sold this ancient secret of his race to Julius Caesar, divided each of the 30-degree divisions of the ecliptic by one of these numbers in succession, which gave them "JHVH, JHVH, JHVH," the triple Godhead or Trinity. Rearranging these letters into "HJH HVVH VJHJH" (this should be written in Hebrew letters), they saw before them the wonderful definition of the G. A. O. T. U., which has come ringing down the centuries. *"He that was," "He that is,"* and *"He that will be"* in 3, 4, and 5 letters (the formula of the 47th problem).

We have already given the formula of *Shamash,* the Babylonian Sun-god, as the physical envelop of the purely spiritual JHVH (640 plus 26). The Sign of the Lion, the "Lion of the tribe of Judah," for J 10, U 6, D 4, A 1, H 5, is only another way of making "26," the "House of the Sun." This is the true Masonic East, toward which the earth and all the planetary bodies voyage, in search of life, light, spring, and summer, and from which they turn Westward toward death, darkness, and winter. The Greek and Roman mythologies are only thinly veiled travesties of the great Eastern Nature Mystery cult, and many of the sacred words thereof which we find on ancient monuments, coins, etc., are also numerical cabalisms. One of the greatest of these, the word *Oriens,* the spiritual "East," puts us directly upon the connection; for its numerical value is O 6, R 100, I 10, E 5, N 50, S 200, = 371, which is 365 plus 6, the cabalistic key to the God of ISH-RA-AL ("Man"-"Sun"-"God").

The Lodge on High

As the lodge is an essay to depict the glories of a Temple in miniature, so was the Temple, in its complete form, an attempt to epitomize the magnificence of a universe and display, in dimensions capable of being grasped by the finite mind of man, those infinite splendors which attest the plan of the Creator.

To the ancient Seer, the universe stood as a concrete visible edifice with limits, bounds, and dimensions. That which he did not see had no existence, and consequently, as a realm of nothingness, beyond the region of the fixed stars, was accepted as perfectly reasonable; for out of that same "nothing" had not the tangible universe been achieved in "six day"?

The vast number of measures and dimensions with which Holy Writ is crowded, nay the very association of square and compasses with the sacred volume upon our altar, are testimony of what men once believed concerning the limited and measurable character of the universal Temple, made comprehensible by geometry.

The earthly Temple was the means given by which man, the lesser universe, a creature connected by invisible cords with and swayed by every superior power enthroned in the Cosmos, with God as Ruler, both above and below, might duly comprehend his importance in the scale of creation and realize that he was himself no less the Temple of the Holy Spirit than the heavens above were the Temple of Almighty God. Thus it transpires that the expression relating to a "Lodge on High" is not without meaning; for every station, character, and ritualistic action of the terrestrial Masonic lodge has its counterpart in the heavens.

It is surprising also with what fidelity to astronomy this similitude has been achieved by the makers of Masonry, and we should be powerless to account for it did we not know of the chief part played by astronomy and what Kepler called "her foolish little daughter, Astrology," in the mysticism of a bygone age.

To us the terms "East, West, North, and South" are all based upon the relation of the earth to sun; but the cardinal points of the heavens are fixed points and have been so ever since the signs of the Lion, Eagle, Man, and Bull were called "the columns supporting the four corners of the universe," by the ancient Egyptians.

These are respectively the celestial East, South, West, and North. Naturally the Master's station is in the "house" of the sun, Leo, "the Lion of the tribe of Judah." At his right is the sign of Cancer, which is the astrological "House of the Moon," and as the moon shines with borrowed light, that is to say, stores up "the gold of the sun;" to give it forth at night, this is the natural station of the Treasurer. To the left of the solar Master is Virgo, "day house" of Mercury, who to the ancient Egyptians was Thoth, the secretary of the gods, or as we should say, "the recording angel." This is still the station of the lodge Secretary. Sirius the Dogstar, as Anubis, made a very creditable Senior Deacon.

The peculiar relation of the candidate to the Junior Warden is known to the initiate. The candidate seeks to escape from the dominion of Mars, whose "night house" is Aries the Lamb, the month that the ancient Hebrews called *Abib*, in which the year started upon its course. When Mars is not "domiciled" in Aries, his place is in Scorpio (the Eagle sign) in the south, his "day house." There is a touch of "esoteric Buddhism" here too; for, to the Hindu philosopher, Mars represented *Kama*, the "desire body" of man, the seat of passions and lusts of the flesh. This unruly element was symbolized as a warrior, sword in hand, prepared to slay the higher promptings of man's better nature. The profound secret of initiation is the subjection of this lower personality and its raising to the sublime degree of master of self instead of its slave. Hence the work of regeneration requires that the man governed by Mars be divested of his sword, that he may not undo the efforts exerted in his behalf by unruliness.

Directly on the other side of the celestial pole, from Leo in the direction of the sign of Aquarius the Waterman, which is the celestial West, is found the constellation Hercules, whose foot rests upon the head of Draconis, the old serpent of death, the ultimate enemy to be conquered. Hercules was to the Tyrians the king of the city, Melkarth, their *Chur Om,* or as the Hebrews called him, *King* Hiram. Hercules, between Leo in the East and Aquarius in the West, stands between the pillars of the solstices. The whole western semicircle of the heavens between Scorpio and Aries is the domain of the three planets of the winter months, ——A, ——O, and ——M, which letters represent Saturn, Mars, and Jupiter, whom the Hindus called Brahma, Shiva, and Vishnu.

Above Taurus and in the direction of the pole lies the celestial domain of Ethiopia, reigned over by King Cepheus and Queen Cassaiopeia, while moored at no great distance lies the good ship Argo Navis, never known to take an unqualified passenger.

Each station of the Zodiac, corresponding to one of the months of our year, has further consideration as a Fellowcraft in the rearing of the Temple of Life, while in the multitude of the fixed stars, each, according to the ancient astrologer, a helpful factor in some part of the "Great Work," if there are not at least 80,000, we shall have to ask the Secretary to read their names again.

The Clothing of a Master Mason

Most of the Masonic eloquence that one hears into which are introduced references to the working tools of the "sublime degree" being wound around their purely spiritual associations, as conceived by the speakers, it is altogether lost sight of that there are practical reasons for the selection of these figures as chief among all symbols of a mystic order, descended from the wisdom religion of the distant past.

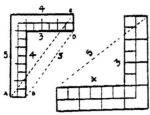

"Operative" and "Speculative" Mason's squares contrasted.

Much can be perceived from an examination of these figures with reference to their relation one to another. There are two squares known to Freemasonry. One is the *speculative* and the other is the *operative* Mason's square.

The operative Mason's square is the true square of Freemasonry and is far more often employed in Masonic symbolism of a bygone age than the other. There are important reasons for this fact. The basic arithmetical quantities of the geometry of self-existent proportions found in nature are the numbers 3, 4, and 5, which, in their simplest combination, constitute the wonderful triangle of our ancient brother Pythagoras.

That which we call an operative Mason's square is as completely natural a figure as the triangle in question, because in addition to its definition of the angle of 90 degrees, the fourth part of a circle, it also lays out the two most important oblongs, those of 3 by 4 and 4 by 5, the angles of which are defined by the dotted lines *b-d* and *a-c*. From myriad applications of these simple figures arose all the sacred proportions employed in planning the tabernacles and Temples of the ancient world.

Our apron is actually an ancient Egyptian geometrical problem, based on the principles of the operative Mason's square, showing a quick and *almost* perfect manner of determining a squared circle, in which the peripheries of both square and circle are of precisely equal length. Correctly dissected, it consists of

111

two oblongs of 3 by 4 (at the top) and two oblongs of 4 by 5 (at bottom). These constitute a perfect square. Setting the immovable point of the compasses upon the intersection of the two lines that divide the square and the free point upon *a* or *b,* we trace a circle the circumference of which is equal to that of the square.

It is not difficult to see that the dimensions of the completed square are 8 by 8, those of the age-old chess or draft board, which we find represented as the game of kings and queens on the oldest Egyptian monuments. Taking the point *c,* the center of the circle, as the situation of the Sun in the center of our universe, and that, as our ancient brethren viewed it, the physical vesture of the Great Architect, JEHOVAH, we can see the application in both square and com-

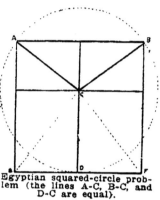

Egyptian squared-circle problem (the lines A-C, B-C, and D-C are equal).

passes, and the clothing of a Master Mason in the fact that the triangle *e-c-f* is the vertical section of the mighty Pyramid of Cheops, erected to perpetuate this self-same design at the remote period of 2170 B. C. The altitude *c-d* is of 10 parts or *Jod,* to a base of the same measure, or *Ha, Vv, Ha,* (5 plus 6 plus 5) constituting the mysterious *Tau* cross of the ancient Israelites.* The derivation of the *speculative* square also becomes plain.

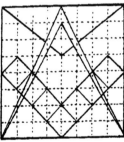

Derivation of symbols of Master Mason.

It has been the writer's privilege to discover the vestiges of the original Magian cult of the Great Architect, or "Builder of the Universe," among the Bactrians of northern India (now called Bokhara), conquered and settled among by Greeks, accompanying Alexander the Great of Macedon.

The Symbolic Trowel

Masonic symbolisms are of two kinds, direct and allusive. The trowel belongs to the first class, because naturally an indispensable instrument of the building art for which an explanation would have to be contrived in any case, in a system based upon architecture. The shape of the trowel, however, is dis-

*See page 95.

tinctive, its blade being of a specialized form, different from any other known tool.

With this shape in mind, examine the outline of the space between square and compasses, usually filled in with the letter G, and it will become apparent that the point of the trowel is an angle of 60 degrees, while its base is one of 90 degrees, in which the handle is set. The moment that this proportion is recognized the outline of the trowel becomes the geometrical basis of the emblematic square and compasses themselves, and the line between the extreme points has the value of the letter *Jod,* the initial of the name of God in Hebrew. As *Jod* represents Spirit acting upon Matter, causing its inchoate particles to cohere in shapely proportions, so the trowel is the instrument employed by master masons to unite fragmentary building material upon symmetrical and orderly plans.

The rescripts ordering the compasses to be open at an angle of 60 degrees, and defining the square as an angle of 90 degrees, are, like countless other Masonic allusions, references to geometrical formulas, well known to our ancient brethren, which have become lost to the craft of today.

A representation of the trowel appears as one of a set of masons' tools displayed on a bronze plate set in the masonry of an ancient building of Thebes, Egypt.

Bactrian Coin of B. C. 180, showing a hierophant of the Magi adoring the Creator under the symbol of an operative Mason's square. The emblem behind him is a Sanskrit monogram of letters, the initials of earth, air, fire, water, ether, and mind, in the sacred language of India.

The Lion in Freemasonry

The several allusions to the "king of beasts" that we encounter in our Masonic ritual are generally accepted as exclusively biblical. This is not, however, the fact.

The great significance of the Lion in all manner of symbolic associations dates from the first inception of the zodiacal system of measuring the heavens and timing the great astronomical cycles, which appointed the sign of a Lion, the fiercest and most redoubtable of beasts, as that of the summer solstice, the moment of the year's most ardent solar vigor.

Speaking as astrologers are wont to express these things, the sign of the Lion is the "House of the Sun," and the terms have thus come to be practically synonymous. It is interesting to Masons who carry the "Lion of the tribe of Judah" as one of the armorial quarterings of their "Royal Arch" banner and on the seals of many Grand Lodges to know that the current Masonic date is arrived at by adding the number of years B. C. (approximately, the true number being 3995) at which the summer solstice entered the sign of the Lion to the year A. D. in which we happen to be.

The truest manner of carrying on the calendar is by means of the slow movement of the equinoctial points round the circle of the ecliptic, which accounts for every instant of time without the necessity of computing leap years and extra months; but in the course of time these points inevitably passed through and out of given signs into their neighbors', which occasioned great confusion, as each time this occurred a disturbance of religious symbolisms with which people had been familiar for several thousand years ensued. In all the cases of which we have record such changes have been made the basis of new religious conceptions which have effected universal revolutions.

The change from the Lion to Crab in B. C. 1835 was the occasion of the organization of the Israelites, the "Tropics" taking, thenceforth, the names of "Cancer" and "Capricorn," and the next change, 2,160 years later, brought out the edict of Constantine the Great declaring Christianity the religion of the Ro-

114

man Empire, for this was the occasion of the great Council of Nice in A. D. 325.

The Hebrew name of the Lion especially relates to this periodical change; for it is ARIH or 1+200+10+5, equalling 216, the digits of 2160, which added together, make 9 or 3 times 3. The God of Israel was the mathematical center of the universe, the point within the circle of the ecliptic, which was supposed to be its outer edge, and His symbolism resided in the "four beasts," which still constitute the arms of the fraternity,—the Lion, Eagle, Bull, and Man, referred to in the first chapter of Ezekiel.

These are the second, fifth, eighth, and eleventh signs, their numbers adding to 26, that of the "Great and Sacred Name" JHVH (*Jehovah*). (See Frontispiece.)

We have frequently had to refer to this number 216 in the course of these papers as the sum of the cubes of 3, 4 and 5 and of the number 6. It is the basis of the ancient names for "man" and "woman," "IshU and IshAH," and is one of the most important numbers of the Hebrew *Kabbalah,* in the depths of which lie buried the nature secrets of which the Thorah gives only the external hints.

Osiris being awakened by Anubis, while his soul hovers above, about to return to the body. Note the bier in the form of a Lion.

The prevalence of this Lion-Eagle-Bull-Man symbol all over the ancient world is proof positive of the contention of the Israelites that at one time all the peoples of the earth worshipped the true God, but with the exception of themselves fell into idolatry.

India, Persia, Babylonia, Assyria, Phenicia, and Egypt all employed these figures in various ways, but especially that of the Lion, which, representing the Sun, was adopted as the symbol of divinely bestowed royalty.

The name of King Solomon, whose throne was approached through an avenue of 12 lions, was composed of the letters S—L—M—N, which as 60—30—40—50 represented the lion cube 2160. All of these things are parts of a huge puzzle which tended to show that no matter in what direction man went or under what aspect man studied the universe, the Great Architect, Jehovah, was always at the center of every situation.

Hailing the risen Horus. Masked Hierophants in the ancient Egyptian Mysteries, from Tomb painting.

Therefore the "Lion of Judah" is no more nor less than the "Lion of JHVH"; for one has only to exchange one of the H's, which is a 5, for DA or 4+1 to see that the word is the same. In the great cosmic year drama of which we have been talking the fruitful principle of nature, slain by the vicissitudes of winter, must be raised to restored vigor and vitality, which is not attained until the young spring sun has attained the sign of the summer solstice. From B. C. 1835 Aries the lamb was the sign of the vernal equinox; while Cancer the crab was that of the summer solstice. The Egyptians made much of this symbolism, because the rise of the Nile and the consequent fertility of their land occurred at the latter period.

Now on the circle of the ecliptic the spring equinox and the summer solstice are just 90 degrees apart. The Egyptians reckoned the speed of the sun at a degree a day; although they lost five days and six hours thereby, which was overtaken at the end of the year. Just two weeks after the summer solstice the wonderful dogstar Sirius, or Anubis as the Egyptians called it, first rose with the sun and at the same time the floodgates of the Nile were loosened. Adding 14 days to 90 gives 104.

Anyone who will take the trouble to examine a map of the heavens will see that the sign of the Crab lies just under the outstretched paw of Leo the lion, while the number 104 is four times 26, one of the most sacred of the old cabalistic formulas. Expressed in *Jod's*, *Ha's*, and *Vn's*, the name of the power that gives new life to nature is JHVH HIH HVVH VIHIH. "Jehovah, who wert, who art, and who ever shall be."

HEREAFTER.   PRESENT.   PAST.   ABSOLUTE.

יָתִית נ:ותְנת:תְהִית:הית:יָהוֹנת:תי

5 10 5 10 6   5 6 6 5   5 10 5   5 6 5 10

WATER.   EARTH.   AIR.   FIRE.

The Secret Formula of the ancient Magi.

The Acacia

The gifted American Assyriologist, Professor Stephen Langdon of Oxford University, recently announced the translation of a clay tablet in the museum of the University of Pennsylvania as a Sumerian declaration, made not less than 5,000 years ago; that Noah, not Adam and Eve, caused the fall of man, by eating the forbidden fruit of the cassia tree. The mystifying discrepancies raised by this curious statement of one of the world's greatest investigators of ancient lore are likewise typical of the vast confusion pertaining to almost everything Masonic; due to the acceptance of theological dogma as authentic history, without analysis as to the origin and purport of the various legends that perpetually clash along the road of time.

If we will but regard the wonderful old Hebrew legends as *versions* of age-old nature myths which achieved expression in analogous legends among other and neighboring Semitic peoples, we shall come closer to historical truth. There is a reason, lying away back at the dawn of human culture for getting Adam and Eve and Noah mixed. This reason cannot be imagined by taking the characters as historical personages, as described in the later writing of the book of Genesis. One must revert to the ancient speculative doctrine of the archetypal, androgynous man, called by the Phenicians "Adam Kadmon," for the true elucidation. These are big and hard words to most of us; but they are the keys to explanations that will be found in good encyclopedias.

Another Assyriologist, translating tablets, announced not long ago that Noah was "a lady"; which seems to make it still worse. Nevertheless there is still a bottom to the mystery, or rather series of connected mysteries; for it is all part of an identical system in the meshes of which we are still unwittingly entangled.

The standard Masonic references to the acacia are principally those of Mackey, who identifies it with the *shittim* wood of Scripture (from which gum arabic is obtained), and of Pike, who says it is the *erica* or thorny tamarisk. Both exhibit well grounded reasons for their contentions, with the burden of evi-

117

dence in favor of the latter, who was an excellent Talmudic scholar. and knew the old Hebrew legends concerning the tamarisk.

The fact is that in ancient *mythos* there is quite a body of arboreal legends, and in the course of time a number of these have become mixed or distorted to fit trees more familiar to certain districts than to those where they originated. The Garden of Eden contained two notable trees, the Tree of Life and the Tree of the Knowledge of Good and Evil. Both of these have become irretrievably mixed among those ignorant of the origin of either. The "Garden of Eden" arose from the ancient Sumerian legend concerning the origin of God's own people —*i. e.*, the Sumerians themselves—in the valley of the Euphrates.

The ancient name of Babylon was *Tin-Tirki* ("Place of the Tree of Life"), and the country round it was called *Kar* (or *Gan*) *Dunyash* (the "Garden of Dunyash") or *Adon Yesha* (the Builder of the Universe), eventually to be called Dionysius or Bacchus. Critical analysis of the Babylonian "Tree of Life," which is depicted in countless archeological remains, shows it to be a representation of the sun and twelve signs of the Zodiac displayed as what are called "palmettes," a fan-shaped figure copied from a palm tree *motif*.

This is not, however, the *acacia* from the Masonic standpoint; yet the latter is contemporary, and will be quickly identified by examination of the cylinder seal called that "of Adda the Scribe," which is No. 89,-

Antique Russo-Greek crucifix, 400 years old, from author's collection. Note the acacia at the bottom. This oriental shape is the foundation of most Masonic Cruciform signs.

115 in the British Museum at London, and about 5,000 years old.

It shows the myth to be that of the "evergreen" in general; which, unlike the other verdure of the earth, does not despair, droop, and wither at the annual death of the sun-god, but announces confidence in his return by retaining her flourishing appearance, when all else in nature seems to have succumbed. The character of the evergreen shrub varies according to locality; but the myth is everywhere the same.

As philosophy progressed, the myriad ramifications of trees suggested mathematical processes, and the conical shape of the conifers, the equilateral triangle of the geometer, and so we find the Angel of the Lord, in the burning bush, paralleled by the head of *Ahura-Mazda*, in the midst of 10 flames, arranged as a Pythagorean *tetrax*, on the Persian fire altars of Sassanian times. So there is also an intimate analogy between the Christmas tree and the 36 *C'Hanukah* candles of the Israelite.

To go back to the question of Adam as the archetypal man, the finest remnant of the old original story that remains to us is one begun in the Talmud and embroidered on by the Byzantine Christians of the time of Constantine. It is as follows:

"When Adam died, his son Seth, before burying him, placed a seed of the Tree of Life, this time the thorny tamarisk, on his tongue. The seed sprouted, burst through the coffin, and grew into a stately tree. When, centuries later, the Roman soldiers were looking for a suitable tree from which to construct the Cross of Calvary, they happened on this particular one, cut it down, and made it the instrument of death. As any object employed in an execution was abhorrent, the crosses were subsequently buried in the spot where the tree had stood, where they remained until the time of Emperor Constantine the Great.

"The mother of this emperor, the pious Helena, dreamed that the spot was revealed to her by heavenly visitants, and thereupon prevailed on her son to send an expedition to Jerusalem to recover the sacred relic. Constantine was so sure of success that he caused beacons to be placed on hilltops all the way from Constantinople to Jerusalem, around his dominions in Asia Minor, to signal back the news of the discovery.

"Singularly enough, it all happened just as Constantine, Helena, and their monkish counselors had figured out. They found the precise locality, disinterred the *three* crosses, and in the course of excavations also recovered *the skull of Adam.*"

This adventure, called in Romish annals the "*Invention of the Cross,*"—and never was a word better adapted to express the truth,—is commemorated by the placing of a tiny skull and crossbones at the base of the Roman Catholic crucifix; but the Greek church displays it, at the foot of its crucifixes, not only the skull, but *a sprig of acacia.*

It was from this Adam's skull tradition that the name *Golgotha* ("Place of the Skull") was derived.

Brother Albert Pike tells us, in "Morals and Dogma" that the "Crown of Thorns" was of this same thorny tamarisk tree. Now another connection must be sought in an old Jewish cabalistic legend also in the Talmud. The latter says that the name "Adam" was spelled "A-D-M," because it thus contained the initials of three successive incarnations of the same spiritual ego, *i. e.,* Adam-David-Messiah. While the facts prove this to be a late rabbinical hypothesis, because the premises are wrong, it nevertheless demonstrates the legendary identity of the archetypal man of primitive legend, the *Adam Kadmon,* with David, who is Thoth, Hermes, or Mercury, and the Messiah, together with the mediaeval notion of an Acacia tree marking the spot where the last should rise from the grave of the first.

The Masonic Symbolism of Color*

The subject of color in connection with Masonry is one which has received very little attention from students, in the past, but it is nevertheless one which is susceptible to some extremely fascinating speculations.

In Symbolic Masonry we encounter reference to but three, the alternating black and white of the Mosaic pavement denoting the "dual principle"; the pure white of the Lily and the Blue color attributed to the Lodge and the Heavens which it is said to imitate in certain particulars. From the latter consideration we derive various notes of blue in lodge regalia and decorations. The Green of the Acacia, though not dwelt upon, supplies the final note on Immortality.

In Capitular Masonry, the prevailing color is Red and much weight is given to the colors of the four Veils, respectively Scarlet, Blue, Purple and White, which are self-evidently representations of those employed in the Tabernacle and subsequent Temples of Israel. Red is the color of Vulcan, god of Fire, whom the Jews called Tubal-Cain and whose number is 9, or 3 times 3.

If we are willing to accept the theory that in the original intention of the sequence of Masonic degrees, "Symbolic" Masonry was to represent the birth, education or development and final test of the perfected soul, and "Capitular" Masonry to symbolize the return of the liberated soul to the source of its being, we shall have no difficulty, whatsoever, in assimilating the presence of these colors in Lodge and Chapter, as indicated, with the ancient Semitic philosophy, in which Old Testament Theology and, consequently, Masonry, had its rise.

The old Chaldean cosmogony, which impressed the Egyptian, Phoenician and Hebrew cults alike, regarded the Soul as a spark of the Divinity, precipitated to Earth, through the spheres of the Seven planets and the Zones of the Four Elements, gathering in the course of its journey, its mental, moral and spiritual attributes from the first group and its physical elements from the second.

The Veils of the Temples were clearly symbolical of the elemental Zones. Water, Fire, Air and Earth, in Hebrew respectively *Iammim, Nour, Rouach* and *Iebeschah*, the initials of

* Originally printed in "The Builder."

121

which words, "I. N. R. I.;" having the numerical value of 10, 50, 200, 10 or 270, gave the cabalistic number of incarnation, founded upon the nine months, of thirty days each, of human gestation and which was also the number of the identified Osiris and Horus, among the Egyptians; the hypothenuse of a right-angle of 162 by 216.

Red stood for the element Fire, Blue for Air, White for Earth, and Purple for Water, the latter, presumably, because purple color was derived from a shell fish, the *Murex Purpurea* of the Tyrians. Their signs were the Lion, Eagle, Bull and Man of Masonic heraldry. The Egyptians, who manufactured colored glass and must have made experiments with light, observing that red and green produced black, made these three colors representative of the J, V. and H. of their secret Supreme Being, HUHI, who was none other than our mighty *Jehovah*. Alternating stripes of Red, Black, Green, Black, standing for the *Tetragrammaton*, being the chief characteristic of the Apron worn by the celebrating Hierophants of the Mysteries of Isis. In their requisitions for Architects to construct their sacred edifices the Hebrews always specified that they be workers in the four symbolic colors and the symbolic metals which also belong to the planetary septenary quoted.

Bezaleel and Aholiab, builders of the Tabernacle in the Wilderness, were "filled with wisdom of heart to execute all manner of work of the engraver, and of the designing weaver and of the embroiderer in blue, and in purple and in scarlet yarn and in linen thread."

The gold, silver and copper employed were respectively sacred to the Sun, Moon and Planet Venus, while the Onyx stone and *Shittim* or Acacia wood, so lavishly employed, were symbols of the planet Mercury, which, to them, became the "Angel of the Lord," *Raphael*.

The celebrated Tyrian Architect, builder of King Solomon's Temple, is likewise described as skillful to work in gold, in silver, in copper and in iron, in stone, in wood, in purple, in blue, in fine linen and in crimson and also to execute any manner of engraving—again a list of symbolic materials embracing the metals of the Sun, Moon, Venus and Mars, the last two indicative of the physical qualities of Attraction and Repulsion, which engender the Vibration which Science is even now identifying as the great cosmic energy.

Many Egyptian sculptures show the figures of Priests holding before the Monarch or the gods, purifying offerings of Fire and Water, the elements of which it was said the Earth had been created and by which it would be destroyed. If, finally, a most delightful theory may be advanced, we would (in our recognition of the advancement of the ancient Seers in many branches of Art and Science which we have only tardily come to justly credit them with), like to presume that part of the universal adoration of Light as the dwelling place of the Deity and the primordial source of substance employed in material creation, consisted in an appreciation of color, as a property of light.

We are perfectly satisfied, that the seven prismatic colors were recognized in the earliest ages of the civilized World. We know that the ancients were acquainted with the manufacture of glass and that in possession of this latter substance, they could scarcely avoid something which is constantly occurring to the astonishment of children, handling glass or crystal in the sunlight, the production of the colors of the rainbow. Why, then, were four colors only selected for the symbols of Matter and the Veils, representing the Elements by our ancient Brethren? All scientists have heard of Wollaston's celebrated experiment, performed in 1801 for the purpose of discovering the ultimate composition of light. We quote the language of his paper in the Philosophical Transactions of the Royal Society of Great Britain in 1802. He says:

"I cannot conclude my observations on the dispersion of light without remarking that the colours, into which a beam of white light is separable by refraction, appear to me to be neither seven, as they are usually seen in the Rainbow, nor reducible by any means, that I can find to three, as some persons have conceived, but that by employing a very narrow pencil of light four primary divisions of the prismatic spectrum may be seen with a degree of distinctness, that I believe has not been described or observed before."

"If a beam of daylight be admitted into a dark room by a crevice, 1-20 of an inch broad, and received by the eye at a distance of ten or twelve feet through a prism of flint glass, free from veins, held near the eye, the beam is seen separated into the four following colors only: Red, a yellowish Green (which might pass as a muddy White), Blue and Violet." The very diagram employed by Wollaston to illustrate this experiment, a human eye viewing the four ultimate colors through a triangular prism, suggests above all things the notion of the all-seeing eye, in the Triangle, viewing His Creation as a compound of the four elements, only known to and symbolized by ancient science.

Red

Light in Masonry

It is indeed worthy of inquiry the character of this illumination that is the object of such ardent pursuit on the part of the candidate, who is as willing today as in the age of the Eleusinian mysteries to brave the terrors of the unknown for its acquirement.

Superficially the term *Light* may be deemed to apply solely to the intellectual enlightenment of one who has hitherto been groping in mental obscurity, with reference to the great questions of man's origin, being, and destiny.

This is not, however, altogether the case. It is often a question as to whether the average initiate in these days emerges from his round of ordeals otherwise than gratified that they are over and that he has gained a right to the coveted fellowship with the elect.

There is a significance in the word *Light* and its fullest interpretation, that far transcends any ordinary sense; for the true promise of "light in Masonry" is the return of man unsullied to the pure source of his being.

Thousands of years before Sir Isaac Newton declared light to be "a subtile form of matter" it was universally accepted as the source of all that was good and beneficent in physical nature. All that exists was deemed to be the product of either the luminous principle in which resided the Godhead, or of the principle of darkness, equally substantial, which waged continual war upon it.

In all the ancient philosophies these two inimical substances engendered and were peopled by beings that partook of their several natures. Man, according to ancient tradition, was originally one of the inhabitants of the Kingdom of Light, and the home story of our first parents, notwithstanding the long-cherished notion of a geographical location for their original site, was among the stars, where they named and presided over the animal-shaped contellations as spirits. The bodies of these were composed entirely of the luminous substance.

The temptation and fall of man has to do with the latter's voluntary commerce with the powers of darkness, or the intermingling of the positive and negative elements, in everything of

124

which we are able to take cognizance through the medium of the senses.

Through this admixture of light and darkness the material world came into existence, and the male and female principle derived from JHVH were driven from the Kingdom of Light to this intermediate region of earth, on which they thenceforth must dwell, "clad in garments of skin"; *i. e.*, in bodies of human flesh.

From that time onward the human soul, according to the intention of the beautiful old Eastern allegory, has been seeking

Initiation in ancient Egypt.

to regain its lost estate ever driven and tempted by the powers of darkness seeking to drag it down to complete and final destruction. We hear less of this story of the connection of Freemasonry with that of the "Fall of Man" than was once the case, when this feature was embodied in the necessary lectures. The candidate, in seeking light, is but seeking his original state of physical innocence, moral integrity, and wisdom. We have in many ways shown that the theater of his endeavors, divested of its cabalistic terms, is our own universe.

With this conception ever in view, and remembering the candidate to be the *Ego,* or self-conscious principle in man, it is easy to follow his spiritual experiences, from the cradle to the evergreen strewn grave, in search of the talismanic word that shall restore his forfeited birthright. It is the Kingdom of Light and the rescue of the body of Light, the original and self-sufficient envelop of the soul, that is the constant object of his search along the rugged road that he is compelled to tread, in quest for the outstretched hand of Him who alone, is able to raise this body from the encumbering matter.

The symbols placed along his path, which at suitable times are interpreted to him, are age-old devices for revealing the mysterious connection between spirit and matter.

The symbolisms of "direction," taken from the points of the compass, in which the solstices and equinoxes were situated at the moment of the inception of the Ancient Mysteries, have served to fix the Celestial East of the summer solstice in the sign of the Lion, as the home and source of perfect light; while its antithesis, the portal of the West, associated with the annual death of Nature, assailed by the blasts of winter, at that solstice, was the station of death, darkness, and dissolution.

It is the destiny of no man to regain the light, unless he face it from the threshold of the great Beyond. There alone will he be invested with the words of power that enable to set at naught temptations, fears, doubt, and error, until, in his final crisis of despair, the Eternal Truth, the Great Architect, the Manifested Word, which is the only authorized substitute for the Unmanifested Word, frees the eternal "Son of Light" from his earthly prison and bids him to the house not made with hands, eternal in the Heavens, whence, as a straying Lamb, he wandered in the infancy of the universe.

This, in short, is a synopsis of the story that Masonry attempts to tell, completed from the wisdom of the ancient East.

FINIS.

HIGGINS' MASONIC MONOGRAPHS

A∴U∴M∴

"THE LOST WORD"

BY

FRANK C. HIGGINS, F. R. N. S.

President of the Magian Society
Past. Pres. N. Y. Numismatic Club
Etc., Etc.

With 22 Illustrations by the Author

PRICE   FIFTY CENTS

BRAHMA.

SHIVA.   VISHNU.

The Great "JOSS" of China, is the Hindu Trimurti, imported,
like Buddhism, from India.

HIGGINS' MASONIC MONOGRAPHS

A.·. U.·. M.·.

"THE LOST WORD"

BY

FRANK C. HIGGINS, F. R. N. S.

President of the Magian Society
Past. Pres. N. Y. Numismatic Club
Etc., Etc.

With 22 Illustrations by the Author

SELECTION FROM "ABT VOGLER"

I

Therefore to whom turn I but to thee, the ineffable Name?
Builder and maker, thou, of houses not made with hands!
What, have fear of change from thee who art ever the same?
Doubt that thy power can fill the heart that thy power expands?
There shall never be one lost good! What was, shall live as before;
The evil is null, is naught, is silence implying sound;
What was good shall be good, with, for evil, so much good more;
On the earth the broken arcs; in the heaven, a perfect round.

II

All we have willed or hoped or dreamed of good shall exist;
Not its semblance, but itself; no beauty, nor good, nor power
Whose voice has gone forth, but each survives for the melodist
When eternity affirms the conception of an hour.
The high that proved too high, the heroic for earth too hard,
The passion that left the ground to lose itself in the sky,
Are music sent up to God by the lover and the bard;
Enough that he heard it once: we shall hear it by-and-by.

—Robert Browning.

A∴ U∴ M∴

The "Lost Word"

It is not so many years ago, that the three simple letters which constitute the title of this essay would have attracted practically no attention at all among thinkers of the Western world.

To-day, on the contrary, they are fraught with interest and speculation, because of the evidences which scholars are continually bringing to light, of their wide distribution over the whole continent of Asia, as either a devotional ejaculation or a symbol to be contemplated with awe and reverence and their equal prevalence in the ancient liturgies of the West as factors to sacred names and words.

To this evidence of ubiquity we are, perhaps, in a position to adduce some testimony, relating to the relative antiquity of a symbol which must have required many centuries to travel so far and assume so many forms as we shall show it to have possessed in the lapse of ages.

The tradition of a word of omnific power in which is concentrated a store of force, at once dynamic and intelligent, so terrific in its intensity that he who knows and understandingly utters it may wield an absolutely divine sway over the powers of the elements, is one of the oldest legends of the human race.

Although the word, supposed to be the one in question, may differ accordingly to race and locality the myths concerning it bear an extraordinary resemblance to each other, for which there should be an acceptable reason however the latter may have been relegated to obscurity during the lapse of ages.

Fig. 1.
"A. U. M."
in Sanskrit.

The almost always luminous Albert Mackey has written of it—"This WORD may be conceived to be a symbol of *Divine Truth* and all its modifications—the loss, the substitution and the recovery are but component parts of the mythical symbol which represents a search after truth. In a general sense, the *Word* itself being then the symbol of *Divine Truth* the narrative of its loss and the search for its recovery becomes a mythical symbol of the decay and loss of the true religion among the ancient nations, at and after the dispersion on the plains of Shinar and of the attempts of the wise men, the philosophers and priests to find and retain it in their secret mysteries and initiations, which have hence been designated as the *Spurious Freemasonry of Antiquity.*"

The final expression quoted, just as it appears in Mackey's Masonic Encyclopaedia, is, however, a type of the complete lack of logical reason which seems to have hitherto pervaded all speculations of this sort. Why spurious? If spurious, Where the genuine?

This sort of speech, to which many of the noblest writers have often descended and still continue to descend in treating of Masonic antiquities, is nothing more nor less than the evasion of an issue which they have felt unable to meet.

We are compelled in contradiction thereof to assert a Freemasonry in antiquity, which was an *actual,* not merely symbolic, repository of the liberal arts and sciences and which taught essential truths by means of figures which came to be afterwards accepted as the symbols of those truths and have now even survived all remembrance of their original associations.

Our direct acquaintance with the symbolic glyph in question is derived from what was probably the land of its original derivation—India. "There", as Albert Pike expresses it, "it represents the three powers combined in the Deity; *Brahma, Vishnu* and *Siva*; or the creating, preserving and destroying powers, *A,* the *first, U* or *oo,* the *second* and *M,* the *third.* All three represented by the mystic character "Y". This word could not be pronounced except by the letters; for its pronunciation as one word was said to make earth tremble and even the Angels of Heaven to quake for fear."

Dr. J. D. Buck, in his most interesting volume *Mystic Masonry,* has a number of observations upon the important role of the triglyph A.U.M. among the ancients.

He lays more stress upon the Hebrew *Tetragrammaton, Jod, Heh, Vau, Heh* as an example of such a Sacred word which "the Hebrews seem to have derived from the Chaldeo—Egyptian Mysteries, which may be traced to the Zoroastrian Fire Philosophy, till *finally* the word is A.U.M. In both Persian or *Zend* and *Sanskrit,* the three letters are found in many names that designate fire—"Flame", "Spirit", "Essence", etc." There is also a closer connection between A.U.M. and the *Tetragrammaton* than has ever been hitherto published as we shall observe in due course. "The symbol of the "Lost Word" of the Master, says Brother Pike, is the A.U.M. of the Persian Magi and the most ancient Brahman, because back of that tri-literal glyph lies the philosophy of the "Secret Doctrine" the synthesis of all knowledge." The *sound* of A.U.M. had not only its profound significance alone but entered into the composition of the Divine Name among many peoples. It is given as the root of the name of the Sun God *Yama*, of the Vedas and *Yang* of the Chinese philosophy.

In Sanscrit it is *Iama*. It is the Chaldean name of the Day (Sun) *Ioma*, the Hebrew *Iom* (Yom) and the first born in the Chaldean philosophy, called *Aoum*, or doubled-*Moum*, the Hindoo "Word of Creation", the Word of Light; '*Om*', '*Aum*', the Sclavonic '*Um*', '*Oum*', meaning 'spirit', 'soul'; '*Ium*', in the Scandinavian Thunder-god's name '*Ium-Ala*', *Iumjo* (*Iumio*) the Thunder-goddess, '*Ami*', '*Ammi*' and '*Ammi Shaddai*'. Hebrew proper names, '*Oma*', the holy fire, in Germa '*Om*' in '*Omanus*' (Ammon,) the Persian Fire-god's name; '*Aom*' in the Hebrew proper names '*Immer*' and '*Aomar*', and the Dorian *Amar*, meaning Day (Mar, the Phoenician Sun); '*Baal-Aum*', '*Ah-iam*', Hebrew names, '*Iam*', day in Egyptian. This old Indo-Germanic Sun-god, *Am*, '*Yama*' in India, '*Yima*' in Persia, '*Euimos*' (Dionysus), '*Am-ons*' in Egypt. In Asia-Minor, his *sacti* or goddess bore his name in feminine form, '*Amma*' and '*Ma*' the Moon; '*Ammia*', '*Amaia*' and '*Maia*', the Earth, '*Ma*' the Egyptian goddess of Truth.

"The word *Aum*, says the *Rama Yana*, represents "the Being of Beings, one substance in three forms, without mode, without quality, without passion, Immense, Incomprehensible, Infinite, Indivisible, Immutable, Incorporeal, Irresistible.

An old passage in the *Purana* says "All the rites ordained in the *Vedas*, the sacrifices to the fire and all other solemn purifications shall pass away, but that which shall never pass away is the word A∴ O-O∴ M∴, for it is the symbol of the Lord of all things."

According to Manu, the figure stands for respectively "Earth," "Sky" and "Heaven."

However, picturesque they may be, the ancient hieratic definitions of symbols seldom lead us anywhere. Those of us who do not receive them *bouche beant,* are irresistably driven to the conclusion that our ancestors who could be so clear on all subjects, when they wanted to be understood, had a, by themselves, well recognized motive when they were so obscure as to be unintelligible.

We may be agreed that A.U.M. represent the three postulates of the Hindu Trinity but there must have been a reason for depicting these in the form of three isolated letters.

One of the greatest hypocrisies ever thrown by artful priest-craft before the feet of credulous humanity and the one over which the most have perhaps stumbled, has been the hypothesis that all the old "paganisms" were simply the devilish inventions of perverted and sinful peoples, unpossessed of the great lights which are the result of special revelations to a favored latter day class.

This assumption is false on the very face. Practically all of the so-called "revelations" with which we of these latter times have anything to do, are filched *in toto* from the same "pagans" who are cursed for having evolved them and, in most cases, we are delivered the ignorantly garbled and misinterpreted details of what, in their original forms were sublime philosophies, in which the propositions, now so obscure and meaningless to ourselves, were expressed in clear and coherent terms which showed the power of primitive men to reason out, from pure induction, many of the same truths which we, of these days, refer to scientists with laboratories, observatories and libraries.

If there is a seeming conflict between Science and Religion, it is because of the trickeries with which all history is filled on the part of the sacerdotal frauds of past ages.

To-day, for instance, we know that the phenomena of Solar and Lunar eclipses are of regular occurrence. We know that their repetitions may be calculated and dates set long in advance.

Those who first gained this knowledge did not, however, freely dispense it. They did not tell the world that they had discovered certain divine laws governing planetary motions, over which they had no more mastery than over the tail of a comet. They abided their time and informed their publics with great pomp and circumstance that they would, on a certain date, prove their control over the dictates of Deity by extinguishing the Sun or the Moon, as the case might be, and reviving it again at will.

The ancient Mexican priesthood, who were accomplished astronomers and knew the planetary movements to an absolute certainty, had their devotees schooled to expect the extinction of the Sun at the end of any fifty-two years, except by their interposition and bloody sacrifices.

All religion began in conceptions of the Divine power and will to do well, evinced in the generally benificent trend of all natural phenomena, but priestcraft reprehended the natural gratitude and direct spontaneous recognition, by man, of the Divine munificence, by libelling Deity as their harnessed creature and a hater, destroyer and torturer of all who bought not their way to favor by substantial earthly tribute collected by the priestly caste and applied to their own gluttonies and aggrandizements.

What has been piously termed "revelation" therefore may be correctly classed as "suppressed discovery" and if we will but once resolutely face the phantoms which glower along the approach to the vision of the God who *Is,* we will discover that the priestcraft of all ages is what has separated man from, not brought him *to* the throne of the Creator.

The great Hindu reformer Rammohun Rai* who lived in the early part of the last century, having acquired an acquaintance with the English language, in addition to Persian, Arabic and his native Bengali, studied the works of Aristotle and Euclid in order to become acquainted with Mathematics and Logic. He then turned his attention to Sanskrit and the Hindu sacred scriptures.

His biographer says "A careful study of the sacred writings of the Hindus convinced him that the prevailing notion of a multiplicity of deities and the superstitious devotion to the licentious and inhuman customs connected with them, were founded in utter ignorance or gross perversion of their religion. The original records inculcated a system of pure Theism which taught the being of *one* God and that it required of its professors a mental rather than an outward worship, with strict personal virtue."

Just as the sacred *Sanskrit* tongue of the Vedas is found to be the root idiom from which the skeletons, at least, of all our Western tongues are derived, showing it to be infinitely more

---

*Founder of the Brahma Somaj.

aged than them all, so our mystic triglyph A.U.M. is manifested as an integral part of so many ancient faiths as to convince us that it represents something closely bound to their common origin and belonging to the philosophy which either preceded or lurked behind exoteric pantheism.

We may inductively reason a number of things which tend to clear the mystery, if mystery there be.

The symbol A. U. M. clearly belongs to a period of inception at which the *Alphabet* had already come into use among the learned classes, if not among the ignorant.

The alphabet undoubtedly first developed as a secret or *hieratic* method of writing, and in all probability in northern India. In the ages during which picture writing prevailed and had begun to be syllabic, the hieroglyph usually represented a double letter, consonant and vowel combined "H" and "A" would not be separately expressed but there would be signs for *Ha, He, Hi, Ho* and *Hu* and even triple letters such as *Chr, Pth* etc. As soon however as we begin to note reference in the ancient cosmogonies to "the Seven primitive sounds," we know that the vowels, pretty much as we utter them to-day, were alluded to. The separation of the vowels from the consonants was the work of clever analysts. Several of them are derived from consonants into the sound of which they inevitably enter.

It is a popular fallacy that the Hebrews did not possess vowels, but only in later years indicated vowel sounds with "masoretic" "points."

The Hebrew language originally employed vowels but in their struggle for individuality—an overweening desire to be peculiar and unlike the peoples around them, they relegated them out of sight and confined themselves to twenty-two consonants. Notwithstanding this manipulation, it is impossible to credit that the Jews did not take full account of their seemingly missing vowels. No peoples more than they made so much of the Alphabet as the vehicle of mystery concealment, especially in that form known as *Gematria*, whereby words delivered up their secrets as mathematical propositions through use of the letters as numerals.

Speaking of the sacred terminology, by which the ancient Hierophants at once concealed and preserved their Wisdom-religion, H. P. B. says—"The peculiarity of this language was that it could be contained in another, *concealed and not to be perceived, save through the help of special instruction.* Letters and syllabic signs possessing at the same time, the powers and meanings of numbers, of geometrical shapes, pictures or idea-ographs and symbols, the designed scope of which would be determinatively helped out by parables in the shape of narratives or parts of narratives, while also it could be set forth separately, independently and variously by pictures in stone work (Masonry) or in earth constructions. Yet the system of the former in this special department of symbology, the key, namely to the mysteries of astronomy, as connected with those of generation and conception, is now proven identical with those ideas in ancient religions which have developed the phallic element of Theology.

The Jewish system of sacred measures, applied to religious symbols, is the same, so far as geometrical and numerical combinations go, as those of Greece, Chaldea and Egypt, for it was adopted by the Israelites during the centuries of their slavery and captivity among the two latter nations.''

The Masonic tradition of the ''Lost Word'' is one which need not here be entered into descriptively because it is so eminently familiar to members of the Craft that the merest allusions are sufficient to establish a connection. The conclusions which are reached at the proper points along the succession of degrees are satisfying to most students and yet there is embodied a still deeper significance in certain Masonic terminology the existence of which is nowhere accentuated, commented upon or offered to special attention. It will suffice, at the proper moment after the general argument has been disposed of, to point out the links which so closely bind the Freemasonry of the present with that of the past as to forever dispose of any doubts as to their authenticity.

Whatever may have been the mechanism contrived for the conduct, perpetuation and government of the Masonic craft, as it is known to-day, by the systematic organizers of 1717; its entire symbolism both material and ritualistic puts the student upon a track which leads directly back to the ancient philosophies of the Occident and of the Orient, with the additional force of making it evident, through the clearest analogies, that the dogmas of the world's religions are but crystallizations of philosophical postulates, which had their rise in investigations, along specific lines, of the phenomena of the natural World.

There are shades of difference in the several interpretations of the term ''Word'' as employed in the present connection.

Many contend that it does not mean ''word'' in the orthographic sense but that it is the *corpus* or body of Divine Wisdom condensed to an expression capable of effecting an impression upon the finite mind, only competent to seize in the abstract that of which the concrete fills the Universe.

This conception is aptly expressed by the Greek ''ΛΟΓΟΣ'', or LOGOS, the philosophy of which has been so ably set forth by Philo Judæus of Alexandria and which is the same expression as that used by the writer of ''the Gospel according to St. John'' in saying ''In the beginning was the LOGOS and the LOGOS was with God and the LOGOS *was* God.''

The term so used is, however, the same which must be employed to express a written or spelled word, and indeed an analogy seems to have been established, with all due regard for the immensity of the contrast. Not only do the traditions of such an oral word as that to which we have alluded exist, but, where in the development of the philosophy of creation through a Divine utterance, that of our universe through the instrumentality of the Divine power and intelligence located in the physical envelope of the Sun is intended, the Solar *Logos* is always represented by a human face surrounded by rays and exhibiting a protruding tongue as the symbol or hieroglyph of speech.

This latter type was common, not only to the lands bordering on the Mediterranean, in most ancient times, but to the early peoples of the American continents especially between Mexico and Peru.

The modifications or transpositions of sacred nomenclatures as they passed from one race to another were generally cleverly accomplished so as to assimilate their esoteric qualities with symbolic *formulae* of local significance. In those of the peoples resident in lands bordering the Mediterranean the influence of Egyptian ideas was exceptionally strong. Practically all the Greek astronomical names are of Egyptian origin and many of the names of gods included in the varied pantheon of *Hellas* are Egyptian or Chaldean as well.

Jove is the *Tetragrammaton*; *Venus*, the *Binah* of the Hebrew *Sepiroth*; *Hermes, Hur-Mse*, the ''Son of Horus''; *Dionysos, Adon Yesha*, the *Dunyash* of Babylon. These are only a few typical cases. A vast lexicon could be constructed of the many examples of this process as between all of the old culture lands.

All the ancient cosmogonies are geometrical projections beginning with the very first verse of the first chapter of Genesis where ALHIM, (*Elohim*) the *Pi* proportion, creates the Heaven and the Earth.

By the Chinese we are given, as the glyph of the mating of light and darkness, in the act of creation of the material universe, the symbol of *Yang* and *Yin,* "the Spirit of God moving upon the face of the Waters," envolving order from chaos. "The Yang appears most perfect in the Sun. *Yang* and *Yin* both arise from the one Primitive stuff. The Divine essence is duality, but the Hindoos say that the Sun is all that is movable or immovable. This whole world has emanated from the Sun. It will return to the Sun, to find annihilation in it."*

Fig. 2. "Yang" and "Yin."

There are many reasons to believe that such of the Hebrew Consonants as were equivalent to vowels such as *Aleph* (א), *Heh* (ה), *Jod* (י), *Vau* (ו), and sometimes *Ayin* (ע), were implied and counted as pronounced, although purposely left out of the spelling. The vowels were closely associated both in Egypt and Israel with the two forms of the Ineffable Name, "HUHI" and "JHVH" which were the same words reversed, just as the Egyptian name "BES" was a reversal of the Semitic "SHEB", meaning Saturn or *Kronos* and it is open to grave question as to whether the Ineffable name is not composed of the vowels above, employed partly as consonants and partly as vowels.

We are not endeavoring to mystify, but we are groping our way toilsomely and with very little contemporary light, through ages during which mystification was the principal business of the learned classes. We find neighboring peoples making gods out of each other's devils and devils out of each other's gods. We find certain races capturing the whole pantheons of other peoples and attempting to transmogrify them into something of their own by spelling their names backwards or awry. We witness the syncretism or blending together of the divinities,

---

*Dunlap.

dogmas and philosophies of several peoples, after a unification by alliance or conquest and the new products bear names which are beautiful combinations of both.

We realize that this could not have been done with historical characters, but where the gods were but anthropomorphizations of philosophical theses, mathematical, astronomical or geometrical verities, the *facts* were identical and the assimilation of names easy enough.

The vowels were, to the ancients, particularly symbolical of the life principle—the breath—inhaled and exhaled, and a word made entirely of vowels, especially if it contained them all, would be particularly expressive of the Giver of Life.

We modern dwellers in the Occident are the only generation of earth inhabitants who have adopted a trinitarian theology without being able to tell what we mean by it or to give it sensible philosophical definition. All of the old philosophies of East, West, North and South recognized the trinitarian aspects of every perceptable phase of "Being." Everything imaginable was and is composed of at least one thing acting upon an-

BRAHMA   VISHNU   SHIVA
THE HINDU TRIMURTI.

Brahma's four heads face East, West, North and South to the Solstitial and Equinoctial points.*

other and engendering a third postulate thereby. Only in God do we find indivisible unity but even that, from our own relative

*The derivation of these three names is fully treated of in the Author's larger work, "Origins and Symbols of Masonry."

standpoint is divided into "Was, Is and Shall be". So far as our perceptable, ponderable world is concerned, the triple nature of every manifestation of Divine power is too palpable to require insistance. The ancients so divided everything, in order to be able to grasp essential truths. What was called the "Dual principle" really resolved itself into a "triple" principle, because every pair of mated opposites produced a "ternary", partaking of the nature of both and yet impossible as the offspring of one alone.

If the old trinitarian philosophies be compared, they will be found to differ superficially, but to be firmly bound together fundamentally.

The Creator is *three;* Knowledge, Power and Perfection or "Wisdom, Strength and Beauty", as it is sometimes expressed. His mode of existence is triple: In the past, the present and the future. In order to create; He becomes Creator, Manifester or Preserver and Transformer or Destroyer. In sex, He is Male, Female, Progeny; In Nature, Spirit, Matter and Spirit *plus* Matter *i.e.* living organism; In spiritual manifestation, Incomprehensible, Comprehensible and Mysterious; In material manifestation, positive, negative and intervibratory, as in Electricity; Physically, Tangible, Intangible and Demonstrable.

Thus did the Sages of old reason among themselves and finding in the internal properties of mathematics and geometry, a mechanical development of the Divine Wisdom which graphically illustrated every formulation of the human intellect concerning it, they sought in applications of mathematical and geometrical verities, to visualize and record fugitive glimpses of the working of the Divine Mind so that their visions of the Infinite might become transmissable and comprehensible to future ages.

We of this Twentieth century, who have not only fathomed the depths of space, but grasped and formulated myriad physical laws, which, though we daily discover variations in their applications, are by every such variation proven to be manifestations of the fundamental and unchangeable ONE, are still like foolish children, when it is proposed to us to seek to apply some of the truths we have learned to a better comprehension of the Infinite.

All Nature proclaims the character of the Omnipotent not only as Creator but as Sustainer and Transformer.

There is not a single law of God which requires a threat behind it to make it binding upon those of mankind who will deign to reason from cause to effect or from effect back to cause. As an advanced soul has formulated

"A thing is not good because God ordains it
God ordains it because it is good."

The conflict of Science is not with Religion, which is of the Heart and is as surely fostered by every fresh revelation of the wonderful resources of Nature as by the promptings of Creeds, but with *Theologies,* which having assumed the authority of exact Sciences, should be as prepared to defend their every presumption as any other branches of learning, the last thing in the world they propose to do.

The glorification of ignorant dogmatisms and hollow sophistries, upon which such so-called Theologies as have the effrontery to set themselves in opposition to ascertained physical truths are built, is unparalleled in any other region of observation.

It is not perhaps necessary for us to here enter upon a detailed account of the causes and motives which have led to the maintenance of such systems in the face of the World's growing knowledge. It is bad enough to know they continue to exist.

It is of paramount importance, however, to realize that the palpable fables, myths and folk-lore stories with which teem the sacred writings of all peoples, were put there for the express purpose for which they have served, that of leading the intellectually unfit astray, in order that they might not fathom the wisdom of Initiates in the hidden mysteries which such material served to conceal.

In their inceptions, every ancient Gospel was accompanied by an oral *gnosis* which was transmitted from generation to generation, by mouth to ear. The written allegories might be freely circulated. The mere fact that they were so circulated, is a certain proof that they contained nothing which their authors feared to reveal to the multitude, or, at least, that their fundamental truths were so completely veiled that it might be assumed that they would remain forever undiscovered in the absence of the *Keys.*

These elaborate precautions, designed in first instance to protect the acquired secrets of Nature—*per se,* of God, from the profane, were the unfortunate cause of a gradual transmission of formulated Theologies from the custodianship of profoundly learned adepts to that of ignorant fanatics. They resulted, when theological primacy came to rest upon political force, in literal interpretations, under the lash of anathemas, of passages which those who wielded the lash, understood the least of all. The reticence of the majority of mankind to pry into that which they were assured were the jealously guarded secrets of a fearsome Creator, can only, on the whole, be commended as inspired by worthy impulses, but this docility was not engendered by the same pure motives as have guaranteed its maintenance during long centuries. The "Masses" were to be docile uniquely that they might be hoodwinked and plundered by "Classes", none more shameless and rapacious than the selfsame "Theologians", who have posed as the Heaven appointed custodians of the "Word". The loving altruism of the Galilean Essenes, has been perverted to rival, in its time, the bloodiest fanaticisms of the most degraded Pagan races. No African Witch Doctor, drinking the blood of his victims from human skulls or aboriginal Medicine Man performing his weird incantations around a slowly roasting captive, has ever sounded the depths of human cruelty and fiendish gore-lust more completely than mitred Bishops and cowled Monks, gathered beneath the standard of a crucified Redeemer, whose dying words are recorded as phrases of mercy and forgiveness.

With the reassertion of the manhood of the human race has come a cessation of the worst features of theological despotism, but the latter is dying hard and struggling in its moribund throes to assert an ascendancy founded upon no higher claims than hierarchial descent from the heretic burners of the Middle Ages and philosophical presumptions, less reasonable than those for which the Law often fines and incarcerates the Clairvoyant, the Astrologer, the Fortune Teller and the Palmist.

The task of the present age is to awaken public sentiment to the fact that these leeches and parasites are but traders in sacred things, as the lawyer who employs the law of the land for the perpetration of injustices, the chemist who uses scientific knowledge to establish drug vices in a community or the merchant whose gains are based on the adulterants he uses. The truth is that there are no mysteries except the One all pervading and ever present mystery, which each individual seeker for union of the segregated mind with the Universal Mind, may fathom for him or herself—"Without money and without price."

The latest dictum of human Science is that MIND is the sole existence and that MATTER is but the concentrated energy of Infinite Mind, moulded for longer or shorter periods into perceptible forms predetermined by Infinite Mind. In other words—Our most modern and recent discoveries, in the realm of physics, lead us directly back to the inspired teachings of the Sages of perhaps ten thousand years ago and our sacred books—our "Bibles" if we will, are not mere manuals of ghostly legerdemain or goblin antics whether of saints or demons, but cabalistic documents having as their bases the ascertainable, ponderable facts of material existence, proving the spirituality of their authors, not as the most tremendous liars of ages past, but as inspired by the possession of demonstrable knowledge, so deep and precise, that they were impelled to preserve it for future ages, under veils which are only now beginning to be rent by the unerring hand of Science.

Every little while, the scandal provoked by some recalcitrant candidate for sacred office, called to give satisfactory proof of his "orthodoxy" before a board of Examiners, belonging to one or another current cult, brings us to our senses, in contemplation of men who are being goaded to accept the doctrines of the "Witch Doctors" and "Medicine Men" of the past, in order to be deemed fit pastors of the Souls of today.

By no contemplation are we brought so completely face to face with the irreconciliable conflict which exists between man made Theology and the "Facts of Infinite Being" as in that of the genesis of the mystic triglyph A.U.M.

To return to the Alphabetical relations of these three isolated letters, we are compelled to recognize them as the first, thirteenth and twenty-sixth letters of a twenty-six letter alphabet, such as the Greek undoubtedly and its Phoenician prototype probably was. Their uses in other connections have shown us the intimate relation of numbers used as letters and letters used as numbers in the construction of sacred nomenclatures, by the peoples of antiquity. Why not follow out the clue here given by the connections of our triglyph, both with our Vedic trinity and its possible numerical significance. If we divide the twenty-six letters of the original Greek alphabet into two equal parts, we procure two rows—from "A", the first, to "M" the thirteenth and from "N", the fourteenth to "Ω" the twenty-sixth, giving us a group of letters which we cannot help at once recognizing as those ever present, to the exclusion of all others, in the deity nomenclatures of the most widely diversified times and places.

In M-A-N-Ω, we have the title of the earliest legendary law-giver of the natives of Hindostan and in N-Ω-M-A, that of the Romans. In Egypt A-M-Ω-N was "the secret one", "the search-er of all souls." The letters "A-Ω" as the *Alpha* and *Omega* of the Greek Alphabet are quoted four times in the book of Reve-lations as the mystical title of the Almighty—"the Beginning and the End", "He that was, is and is to come" and the letters "M" and "N" supplied the nomenclature of the celebrated Theban statues of the "Dual Principle", Mem-Non, also symbo-lized by the Egyptians as a fish swimming in water, or spirit circulating through matter.

We have already written extensively in support of our con-tention that all dogma has been at one time or another reasoned out of purely material phenomena, not with the intention of demonstrating the finality of materialism but, in that of show-ing infinite mind and conscious intention to lie behind all that is physically perceptable.

The "God geometrizes" of the Greek philosopher, Plato, was not a mere passing observation, but epitomized in two words the secret basis of the faith of the entire ancient world. No, however logical thinker, untutored in, at least, the rudiments of geometry, can form the slightest notion of the wonders of this first and noblest of the sciences, as revealed to the discerning mind. Geometry is so close to God that it is the one, unique and indispensable transformer by which *Chaos* resolves itself into *Order*. It is the foundation of all perceptable Nature, present in all that exists and obeyed even by those imperceptable ele-ments which we term "forces" in that they are confined by the boundaries it imposes and can only manifest themselves accord-ing to its immutable laws.

The language of Geometry, that is to say, the manner in which we make our perceptions of its verities intelligible to each other, was discovered ages ago. It can hardly even be said to have been "discovered" for the division of a circle into three hundred and sixty degrees can be shown to be prescribed by Nature herself.

Evidences exist all over the world of an age long past, when Geometry was considered and adored as the chief manifestation of the divine intelligence—in all events it was the language which God spake and man could understand.

The relations of Geometry to Mathematics and of both to Astronomy, together with the astounding recurrence of certain identical quantities common to all, convinced men that they did not go amiss in basing all of their conceptions of divine law upon those observations and so, in critically examining the otherwise obscure metaphors of the world's oldest scriptures we are driven to the inevitable conclusion that Geometry, Mathematics and Astronomy are their common basis.

Furthermore, all ancient religious symbolisms, either obsolete or descended to our day, prove to be derived from geometrical problems. Not merely as forms, but as the Keys to interesting problems which filled the ancient mind with reverence and awe.

A thousand years before Archimedes of Syracuse declared the formula 3.1415 to express the relation between a circle and its diameter, the pious scribe who penned the first verse of the first chapter of Genesis, had embodied it in the the mystic word ALHIM* (אלהים) which has descended to us as "Elohim".

The wonders of the "Pythagorean proposition", called by later writers the "Forty Seventh problem of Euclid" because of its embodiment in that ancient text book, were responsible for practically all the other biblical names of Deity, while the greatest of all, that of the Lord God of Israel, the Ineffable *Tetragrammaton* (יהוה), is the direct derivation from a triangle which sets forth a relation of the square to the circle and is the fundamental geometrical principle of the Great Pyramid of Gizeh, in Egypt.

The name of ABRAM, derived from the BRAMA of India, carries with it the philosophy of the square of the number twelve, or 144, viewed as the great basic truth for which all nations sought and which was represented by the famous Breastplate of the Jewish High Priest.

Our sacred triglyph A.U.M., probably the oldest of all, is also representative of an ancient philosophy of basic truth, as expressing, in one and the same syllable, the conception of Deity

*In the beginning God (Alhim) created the Heaven and the Earth and the Earth was without form and void.

as Creator, Maintainer and Transformer and of Geometry as the connecting link between Spirit and Matter—the modius by which the mental conceptions of the former become manifest in the latter.

Let us approach this conception of the derivation of A.U.M. by the examination of a problem designed to demonstrate the following important geometrical laws. (Fig. 3.) 1. That only a right angle triangle may be inscribed within a semicircle of which the diameter constitutes one side. 2. That the radius of a circle constitutes the chord of an arc equal to one sixth of its circumference, or sixty degrees. 3. That the circumference of a circle is (in rough computation) three and one-seventh times its diameter.

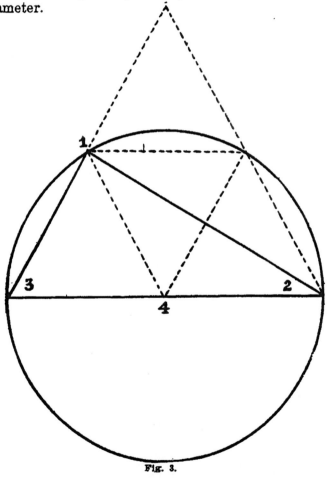

Fig. 3.

The first assumption proves itself. The second is proven by the equality of the lines—1-3, 1-4 and 3-4 which constitute an equilateral triangle while the whole triangle 1-2-3 is one half of an equilateral triangle and presents angles of 30, 90 and 60 degrees.

Fig. 4. Egyptian hieroglyph representing the Sun and the Horizon, which upon analysis proves to be a **reductio** of the problems herein dealt with.

The third proposition brings us to a very interesting problem which is the subject of an important though hitherto unrecognized hieroglyph of the ancient Egyptians.

An oblong square of 14×8 (7×4) dimensions has, among several extraordinary geometrical properties, the fact that one of its longer sides constitutes the precise diameter of a circle, the perimeter of which equals that of the oblong in question. This oblong, (H-B-D-E) is readily reducible to a square because the length of its perimeter being

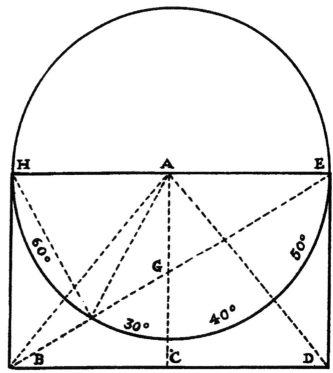

Figure 5. The Geometrical correspondences of the oblong of 4 x 7.
Representations of this problem adorned the frieze and pillars of the great Temple of Denderah, Egypt.

$14+8+14+8=44$, it is equal to 11 by 11. It must be remembered that this is not primarily a question of areas but

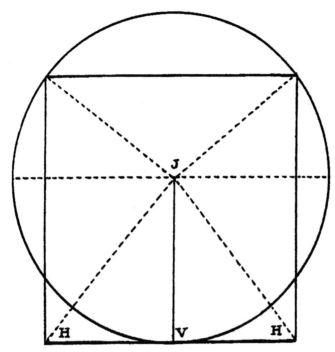

Fig. 6. The foregoing circle with the oblong squared. See "The Apron" by Author.

of perimeters, but this problem throws strongly into relief the famous forty-seventh problem of Euclid, for the triangle A-B-C-D exhibits the base of a square (B-D) and the radius of a circle (A-C) of equal Area while the triangle J-H-V-H exhibits the base of a square (H-V-H) and the radius of a circle (J-V) of equal perimeter, thus showing the fundamental identity of the *gnosis* of all the ancient peoples, who employed one or another of these figures as sacred symbols.

There are many considerations of absorbing interest to the geometrician and the symbolist in the relative proportions of the natural intersections of the lines of Figure 5, which need not be entered upon here. The object of the diagrams given, is to accentuate the fact that *the number 14 represented the value of the diameter of the Circle.* The Hebrew אלהים (ALHIM) or "Elohim" representing 3.1415, has cabalistically this significance as also denoting 3+1+4+1+5=14. Returning to Figure 3 and according to the diameter (3-4-2) the value of 14 parts, the chord, 1-3, being equal to the half diameter or *radius,* will necessarily represent 7 of the same parts, while upon careful measurement the line 1-2 will be found to contain a slight fraction over 12 of the same parts. Comparison will also show the close identity of the triangle 1-2-3 of Figure 3 with the triangles H-B-E and B-E-D of Figure 5.

Geometricians armed with modern high power micrometers may find minute differences, but we are dealing with the measurements of our ancient brethren who considered themselves in the presence of wondrous coincidences.

We have a number of wonderful examples of the employment of this triangle of 30°—60°—90°, inscribed within a circle, as representative of profound metaphysical notions. For instance, to quote from the "Book of the Master" by W. Marsham Adams, "A notable feature of the Great Pyramid of Gizeh, is

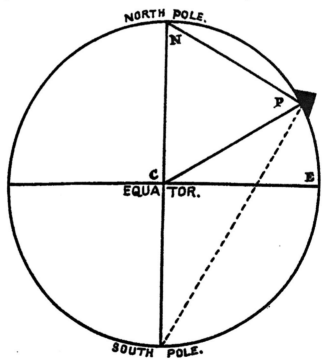

Fig. 7. Geographical situation of the Great Pyramid of Gizeh as a monument to the known science of the time of its erection.

the situation of this building in its relation to the two principal points to which all human measurements of space must be primarily referred, namely the centre and the pole of the earth, since its distance from the pole is just equal to its distance from the centre''.

This property may perhaps be clear from the following considerations. Suppose C to be the centre of the earth, P the situation of the Great Pyramid, N the North Pole, and E the point where the meridian of the building cuts the Equator, then E-C-P will be the latitude of the building, 30°, whence it will be seen at once that the triangle C-N-P will be equilateral, since the angle at C is 60° and the radii C-N and C-P will be equal to each other, assuming the earth to be a sphere.

Hence, therefore P-N, the distance of the Pyramid to the North Pole will be equal to P-C the distance to the centre of the earth.'' It is notable that the very pyramid which still stands as a monument to the mathematical, geometrical and astronomical wisdom of the ancient Egyptians, has, as its vertical axis, the same ·triangle (J-H-V-H) which is represented in Figure 6. (See ''*The Apron*.'' by Author.)

Equally curious was the manner in which this 30°-60°-90° triangle was applied, presumably by the Egyptians, to the three sacred phases of the Sun. Quoting the learned Adams again— ''I am *Tmu* in the morning'' says the Creator in a well known passage, (Hymn to *Amun Ra*), ''*Ra* at noon and *Harmachus* in the evening'', that is to say the Dawn, the Noon and the Sunset are three distinct forms, coexisting perpetually and co-equally in the substance of the Sun, so also did the three divine persons co-exist perpetually and co-equally in the substance of the uncreated Light. This hymn, after declaring the sacred Unity, in the most emphatic and explicit terms, proceeds to invoke the three persons by name (*Amun*) using, nevertheless, the singular pronoun for the collective three, precisely as Abram does, when visited by the Deity on the plain of Mamre (Genesis XVIII, 1-33). The Hebrew Solar name of Deity was extremely similar to this, being ''AL-OM-JAH.''

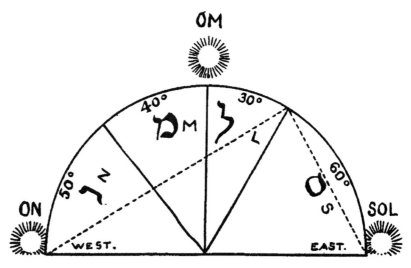

Fig. 8. "THE WISDOM OF SOLOMON."

The effect of this division of the semi-circle is precisely that of the preceding one (Fig. 5), except that it is an amplification thereof. We have not only the Pyramid marked apex, but as the first ninety degrees have been divided into two parts, of 60° and 30° each, so the second half is divided into 40° and 50°, the authority for which we will discover in the natural intersections of the former figure.

For the interpretation of this we must turn to the *Gematria* of the Hebrew language, in which each number is represented by a letter of the Alphabet and we at once discover that 60 is *Samech* (ס) or "S", thirty *Lamed* (ל) or "L", Forty, *Mem* (מ) or "M" and Fifty, *Nun* (נ) or "N", a skeleton of S—L—M—N, which, when filled in with the three mystic "sixes"—6×6×6=216, the cube of "six" and the sum of the cubes of 3, 4 and 5 and 666, the grand numbers of the Sun, are bound up with all the ancient solar mythologies of the Orient. "SOLOMON" thus stands for "SOL" the Rising Sun, "OM", the Sun at Meridian, and "ON," the setting sun, and stands revealed as the son of D—4, A—1, V—6, I—10 and D—4 or 25, the number of "the Square on the Hypotheneuse" of the sacred Pythagorean triangle, (*Horus*), but, in the present case, DAV—11 the side of the square and ID—14 the radius of the circle. It may be argued that these two spellings although incorporated in our English Bible are not equivalent to the original Hebrew שלמה, *Shlmh* and דוד DUD (a form of *Thoth*) but we have our names verbatim from the Aegypto-Greek *Pentateuch* and evidences are multiplying daily that the Hebrew religion of יהוה was not original with the *Beni Yishral,* but was a geometrical variation upon themes selected by their early leaders from the ancient wisdom of the Hindus, Chaldeans and Egyptians.

Fig. 9. The Three Rays of the Druids and Chaldeans.

Fig. 10. The Hebrew letter **Shin,** symbol of the Sun.

We have accentuated our conviction that the Alphabet of Greek and Hebrew, coinciding in so many important particulars, are the descendants, but little changed of a most ancient sacerdotal system. By use of the Alphabet in practically its present Greek and Hebrew forms, it is possible to as intelligently interpret the mathematical, geometrical and astronomical significances of many ancient Sanskrit, Chaldean and Phoenician sacred names as of those of the before mentioned peoples.

There are reasons (See Origins and Symbols of Masonry, by the writer) for believing the Greek Alphabet of *twenty-six* letters to be this ancient sacred system in practically its original form. Twenty-six is the sacred number of the *Logos,* the *Evohé Adonis* of the Eleusenian Mysteries of Greece and Syria.

Remembering now, the standardized values of our Key triangle of 30°, 60°, 90°, we, starting at the apex with the letter A,

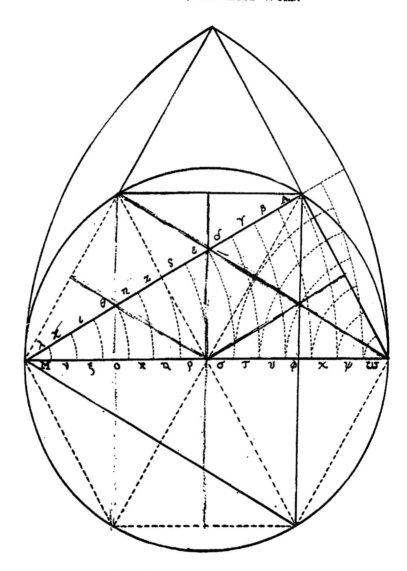

Fig. 11. The "Word" in the Egg.

"In these three persons the one God is shown,
Each first in place, each last, not one alone,
Of Siva, Vishnu, Brahma, each may be,
First, Second, Third, among the Blessed Three."
—Hindoo Poem.

(Fig. 11), apply one to each of the twelve spaces of the top line
and the remaining fourteen to the diameter.

Is our result not clearly to exhibit the letters "A", "U" (OO or Ω) and "M", as the alphabetical representatives of the triangle under consideration?

Having been given to realize the supreme importance in which this triangle was held and its manifold applications to the deepest metaphysical penetrations of every age, we now understand what is meant by the omnific word which ordered the Universe into *Being* by creating a form which lies at the root of its every manifestation. "A" as *Brama* is the Creative Beginning, "M" as *Vishnu* is the Manifesting Center and "Ω" as *Shiva* the transforming end. Between *Alpha* and *Omega*, "the

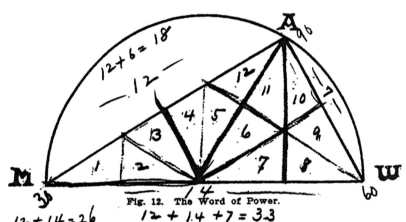

Fig. 12. The Word of Power.

beginning and the end", are the mystic *Seven*, all that mysticism has associated throughout the ages with this patent number, the Planets of the *Sabaoth*, the *Rishis* of India, the prismatic Colors, Metals, Notes of Music, Vowels, and all the other wonderful attributes to the Septenary, down to the seven stars held in the hand of the "Son of Man."

The influence of this age old system is felt to this day throughout the whole fabric of the Christian Religion and of Masonic institutions.

The all embracing *Alpha* and *Omega* together with the fact that His mystic letter was "M",* identifies the incarnation of the philosophic *Vishnu*, who was at once *Chrishna* and the *Christos*, He whom the Roman mystics called the *Artifex Uni-*

*"The most sacred of all is the letter "M" says H. P. B. It is both feminine and masculine, or androgyne, and is made to symbolize Water in its origin. It is a mystic letter in all languages, Eastern and Western."

versus Mundi and of whom they said, transposing the letters to "AMO", "God is Love", whence *"Horus"* became *"Eros"*. *"Anu"* was the Chaldean "I Am", later the "AHIH AShR AHIH" of the Hebrew, the *Nuk pu Nuk* of the Egyptian.

Fiz. 13. Hoti Indian (Arizona, U. S. A.) baked clay Triad called by them "The Three Wise Men." The symbolisms are clearly those of Brahma, Vishnu and Shiva. At the feet of the centre figure (hidden) is a papoose. Below, the symbol of Clouds and Water or "Heaven and Earth."

Even to this day, Christian worship is continually broken with an invocation to A M U N (*Amen*), of which the reason is completely ignored and unknown.

The name of the "Eternal City" contains the omnific word as a combination of "OM" and "RA" which reverses into the name conferred by the Romans upon *Horus* or *Eros*, AMOR. This was indeed no novelty for it closely tallied with *Amar* the Doric name for "Day" in the Solar sense.

The Amorites named their province from the same motive, for all these words are, at bottom, so many terms for the orb of day.

The Greek word, HELIOS, for the Sun, has like IRIS, the Rainbow, the numerical value of the 180° of the Solar arc and combines the *Tetragrammaton*, IHOH, with the Numerals 60 and 30. It is true that the phonetic roots are taken from elsewhere, but idleness was not one of the sins of the old mystery makers.

"The Phoenicians considered, that as the light proceeding from the Sun is the source of life, it is also a spiritual influence and poetical power.*

Mahan Atma, the great Soul or Spirit of the Hindoos is the Sun and Brahma.

From *Aman*, the Sun are taken—AMUN, in Egypt the Demiurgic or world creating spirit and a Hebrew word meaning "Builder". The word "OM" enters into names of the Sun in India, Greece, Palestine, Egypt, Asia Minor and Chaldea.

---

*Movers. †Weber.

"ON"‡ is Chaldean, Syriac, Phoenician and Egyptian for the Sun. The fish god of the Phoenicians was "DAG (a fish) ON". The Hebrew Melkarth or Hercules was SHAMASH-ON, "Samson", the Egyptian name of Heliopolis, "the city of the Sun", called by the Jews *Beth Shemesh*, was ON.

The very name of "Man" is derived through a chain of correlatives from the Sanskrit *Manas*, "*Mind*" and that from *Manudscha*, "the Sun born."

"The Heart of the Universe, (Brahma) excited by Love (*Kama, Eros, Amor*) becomes creative" say the Hindoos, "and from it the senses emanate, changing the space within the *Manas*, (the Divine Mind or Soul) into the external world. The world emanates thus from Brahm.†

The "Supreme Wisdom" of the Egyptians was *Thoth* who to the Hebrew symbolistis became *Daud* or David and the same "Divine Wisdom" was the LOGOS (Sol, 3-6) of Plato, Philo and St. John.

"The teaching of the Brahmans was that Brahm, the Soul of the World, shone forth in person and pronouncing the word "AUM", the Mighty Power, became half male, half female.

"All of the more western triads or three-fold conceptions of the Solar Nature god are in complete agreement with the Brahmanic trinity of *Brama, Vishnu* and *Shiva*, the Creator, Preserver, Destroyer."

They represent at once the yearly aspects of the Sun—the Spring Sun, the Summer Sun and the Winter Sun and the daily aspects, the rising Sun in the East, the Sun at Meridian in the South and the Setting Sun in the West.

The most familiar assimilations, however, are those of *Brahma* to Saturn, *Vishnu* to Jupiter and *Shiva* to Mars.

In the stellar *mythos*, the same characters are associated with the planets so-called, and in every part of the world, including ancient America, have become the legendary *Magoi*, the "three Wise Men" or "three Kings of the East".

Their representations in ancient and Oriental Art are always those of an elderly Sage, one in middle life and a sinster individual of forbidding aspect, generally represented as an armed warrior and most generally a black man. For these the Greeks substituted the "Three Fates."

‡"On", 56 is 26 plus 30. Dividing 30 successively by 10, 5, 6, 5 (J-H-V-H) gives the correct length of the Solar year.
†The "Bosom of Abraham" is still the Semitic figure for the source of all emanation. (Brahm).

Fig. 15. The Visitation of the Magi, the "Three Kings" or "Wise Men of the East." The gifts they bear are those of Brahma, Vishnu and Shiva; The Gold of fortune to the new born, the Frankincense of worldly honor to the adult man and the Myrrh of costly embalming to the fortunate Dead. The symbol of the Lamb is too obvious to require comment. See frontispiece.

In the Book of Zechariah (Zech. III, 1.) they are to be discovered in the famous scene where Jeshua (*Vishnu*) receives the command to rebuild the Temple* and is antagonized by Satan (*Shiva*), lord of Death.

THE MUNDANE EGG.

Intimately connected with the Brahmanic Solar myth is the symbolism of the "Mundane Egg", which is another of the universally disseminated mysteries of obscure Aryan origin. The laws of Manu tell us—

"This universe existed only in darkness, imperceptable, undefinable, undiscoverable by reason, undiscovered as if it were wholly immersed in sleep.

Then the self existing Power, himself undiscovered, but making this world discernable, with fine elements and other principles, resplendant with brilliance, the Most Pure appeared dispelling the darkness.

*The resurrection of the material body.

He, whom the mind alone can perceive, whose essence eludes the external organs, who has no visible parts, who exists from eternity, even he, the Soul of all beings, whom no being can comprehend, shone forth in person.

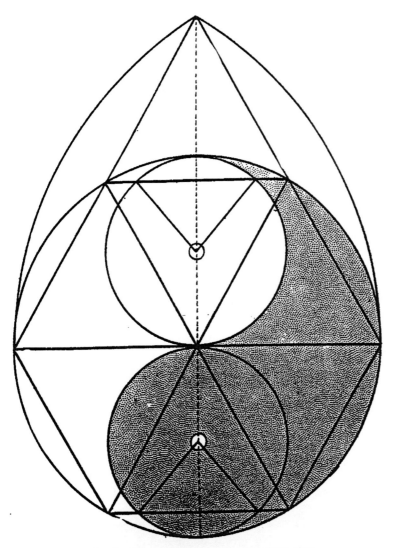

Fig. 15. Brahma (BRAMA) in the Mundane Egg.

He, having willed to produce various beings from his own divine substance, first, with a thought, created the

waters (chaotic matter) and placed in them a productive
seed (The Solar *Logos*).

The seed becoming an Egg, as bright as gold—and in
that Egg he was born himself—BRAHMA, the great fore-
father of all Spirits. By that which is, by the imperceptable Cause, eternal, who really exists and to our perceptions does not exist, has been produced the Divine Male
celebrated in the World under the name BRAHMA.

In that Egg the Divine Power sat *a whole year,* at the
close of which, by his *thought* alone, he caused the Egg to
divide itself, and from its two divisions he framed the Heav-
en and the Earth.''

This is precisely what is indicated by the *Yang* and *Yin*
symbol which represents this very separation of the circle of
Eternity into a semblance of the White and Yolk of an Egg, the
analogy suggested by the physical properties of the *ovum* being
heightened by the self evident application of a geometrical
ellipse to the spherical body of the shell in determining the
actual shape.

The result of this figure is to determine two triangles each
representing the base of the square and radius of the circle of
Equal Area, in fact the A-B-C-D triangle of our Figure 5.
These triangles, united, form a parallelogram of the sacred
oblong of 3 x 4, held by all the ancient peoples as symbolic of

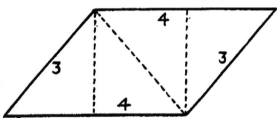

Fig. 16. "The Three fall into Four."

the Universe as it is even now of the Masonic Lodge, and these
proportions, multiplied together, produced the sacred name
3×4×3×4=144, the Square of twelve, or B=2, R=100, A=1,
M=40, A=1=144. It is notable that twelve of these 3 x 4
oblongs constituted the proportions of the Breastplate of the
Jewish High Priest, each stone being related to a sign of the
Zodiac.

The number 144 also relates, esoterically, to the Precession
of the Equinoxes or march of the Vernal Equinox around these
self same Zodiacal signs. Employing the proportions of the

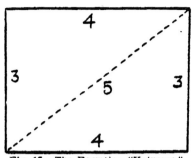

Fig. 17. The Egyptian "Universe."

sacred Triangle 3—4—5, the basis of the great Pythagorean Problem (47th of Euclid), we produce $3 \times 12 = 36$, $4 \times 12 = 48$ and $5 \times 12 = 60$.

Multiplying these figures together, $36 \times 48 \times 60$, we secure 103,680, which is just four times 25,920 Solar years or four complete Precession periods, those upon which all the *Kalpas, Yugas, Kali-Yugas* and other great periods of time were based by the Brahmins. These figures and the geometrical features

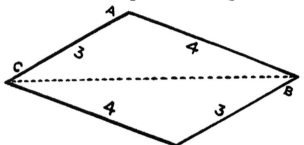

Fig. 18. J-H-V-H (See Fig. 6) C-B, the base of the Square and A-B the radius of the circle of Equal perimeter.

of their production will more than suffice not only to graphically illustrate the evolution of the great Hindoo metaphysical system but also show that it was developed from the self same material in far off India as in Egypt, Chaldea, Palestine and Central America, where its most numerous traces are found.

Among our many evidences that the religions of the West are derived from the Identical Aryan sources which gave rise to the geometrical metaphysics of primitive Brahmanism, we may quote the Orphic Philosophy of ancient Greece which placed "Time", (*Chronos,* who is Saturn and consequently *Sheb* and *Abram*) at the head of all things and endued it with life and creative power.* "Therefore "Time" is God. From Him ema-

*Dunlap.

nates Chaos and Aether, *Chronos* makes an Egg of the Chaos, surrounded by the Aether and from this springs the golden winged *Eros—Phanes* (the Sun). Zeus, according to the Orphic poets is the "Soul of the World".

The unity of Zeus and Eros is established by the Orphic poems as *Chronos Zeus,* God, and *Zeus Eros,* the Spirit of God and this latter is the *Logos,* which was "made Flesh." ("The Father is in me and I in him", John X, 38). Finally the numerical value of the Greek word for God, "ΘΕΟS", is *Th,* 9; *E,* 5; *O,* 70; and *S,* 60 or a total of 144 which precisely corresponds with Brama, Abram and the Jewish Breastplate.

The Orphic Egg is also identified as Hercules (*Erakles*), and the identity of Zeus, Horus and Hercules is most overwhelmingly set forth in the symbolism of Ptolemaic Egypt.

According to Eudemus of Rhodes, a pupil of Aristotle, "The Sidonians set before all, Saturn (Time), Desire (Love) and Mist (the Solar Nebula). "Desire" is the Babylonian *Apason,* the Love of the unrevealed God.

From the union of Desire and Mist (Divine love and the primordial fire mist) were born Aether and Air and from these two, the Egg is formed by the intelligible Wisdom." "The Egg, the Duad of the natures, Male and Female contained in it", said Damascius, "and the third in addition to these is the incorporeal God with golden wings upon his shoulders (the Sun), on his head a serpent invested with the various forms of Animals (the Zodiac). This is the Mind of the *Triad.*"

Eros was the tendency to create. Aether and Chaos, Spirit and Matter constituted the great Phoenician doctrine of the two principles, represented by the globe topped pillars before the porch of the great Temple of *Melkarth* at Tyre and reproduced before that of Solomon's Temple. In fact the two inner circles of the geometrical Egg still surmount the chapters of our columns to-day, with upon their convex surfaces representations of the various parts of the *Earth* and Face of the *Heavens.*

The thoughtful Craftsman will also have experienced little difficulty in recognizing, from the foregoing, what is meant by the three "A", J, J and J, while the Companion of the R. A. (Ra) will now well mark that *three,* not two, symbols constitute, as since it was first given in the caves of Ellora and Elephanta, his M. M. token and the imagery of the "Council".

In various parts of the *Secret Doctrine* and *Isis Unveiled*, by the gifted founder of the original Theosophical Society, H. P. B., as she is familiarly termed, has made many valuable references to the "Mundane Egg" drawn from her extensive review of Oriental Sacred literature.

"Whence this universal symbol?", she asks. "The Egg was incorporated as a sacred sign in the cosmogony of every people on the earth and was revered both on account of its form and of its inner mystery. From the earliest mental conceptions of man, it has been known as that which represented most successfully the origin and secret of "Being." The gradual development of the unperceptable germ within the closed shell; the inward working without any apparent outward interference of force which, from a latent nothing, produced an active something, needing aught save heat and which, having gradually evolved into a concrete, living creature, broke its shell, appearing to the outward senses of all as a self germinated and self created being. All this must have been a standing miracle from the beginning."

"It is owing to the serpent being oviparous that it became a symbol of Wisdom and an emblem of the *Logoi* or self-born.

In the temple of Philae, in Upper Egypt, an egg was artificially prepared, of clay, mixed with various incenses. This. was hatched by a peculiar process and a *Cerastes* or Horned Viper was produced." "In the "Book of the "Dead" reference to the Mundane Egg is often made.

Ra, the Mighty One, remains in his Egg, during the struggle between the "Children of the Rebellion" and *Shu,* the Solar Energy and the Dragon of Darkness.

Fig.19. The Egyptian Crux Ansata, with the Egg. symbol over the Tau.

The Deceased is resplendent in his Egg when he crosses to the land of Mystery. He is the "Egg of Seb" (*Sheb,* Abram, Brahma).

The Egg was the symbol of life in Immortality and Eternity and also the glyph of the generative matrix whereas the *Tau* (T) which was associated with it was only the symbol of life and birth in generation.

The Mundane Egg was placed in *Khoom,* the Water of space or the feminine abstract principle. *Khoom* becoming, with the fall of mankind into generation and phallicism,

AMUN, the Creative God. When *Ptah*, the Fiery God, carries the Mundane Egg in his hand, then the symbolism becomes quite terrestrial and concrete in its significance. In conjunction with the Hawk, the symbol of Osiris—Sun, the symbol is dual and relates to both lives, the mortal and the immortal.

The engraving of a papyrus, in Kircher's *Œdipus Ægyptiacus*, shows an Egg floating above the mummy.

This is the symbol of ''Hope'' and the promise of a second birth for the Osirified Dead. He is ''Soul'', which after due purification in the *Amenti* (purgatory) will gestate in this Egg of Immortality, to be born therefrom into a new life on Earth.''

This is the precise Brahmanic doctrine of the continual passage of the Soul around the three sides of the Triangle representing Creation, Manifestation and Transformation, or return to the first named state.

In the Hindoo myths, ''*Vinata*, a daughter of *Daksha*, and wife of *Kashpaya*, the self-born, sprung from ''Time'' (Again *Chronos, Sheb* the Elder Saturn and Brahma), one of the *seven* creators of our World, brought forth an Egg from which was born *Garuda*, the vehicle of Vishnu, the latter allegory having relation to our Earth, as *Garuda* is the Great Cycle.

The Egg was sacred to Isis and therefore the Priests of Egypt never ate eggs.

Chnum was the modeller of men and things out of the Mundane Egg, on a potter's wheel. *Amun-Ra*, the Generator, is the secondary aspect of the concealed Deity.''

''It is *Kneph* the one supreme planetary principle, who blows the Egg out of his mouth and is therefore Brahma, the shadow of the Deity, Cosmic and Universal, of that which broods over and permeates the Egg with its vivifying spirit until the germ contained in it is ripe, is the mystery God, whose name was unpronounceable. It is *Ptah*, however, the opener of Life and Death, who proceeds from the Egg of the world to begin his dual work.

Fig. 20. Old Hindoo Coin, showing Solar Egg.

''This ''World Egg'' is perhaps one of the most universally adopted symbols, highly suggestive as it is, equally in the spiritual, physiological and cosmological sense.

Therefore it is found in every world theogony, where it is largely associated with the Serpent symbol of the latter, being everywhere in philosophy as a religious symbolism, an emblem of eternity, infinitude, regeneration and rejuvenation as well as of wisdom. The mystery of apparent self generation through its own creative power, repeating in miniature, in the egg, the process of cosmic evolution, both due to heat and moisture under the efflux of the unseen creative spirit, fully justified the selection of this graphic symbol. The ancients represented the latter by a serpent for "*Fohat* hisses as he glides hither and thither, in zigzags." The Kabbalah figures it with the Hebrew letter *Teth,* (ט) (Nine or "Three times Three") whose symbol is the serpent, which played such a prominent part in the Mysteries.

Ain Soph, is called "fiery Soul of the Pelican" in the Book of Numbers. Appearing with every Manvatara as *Narayana* or *Srayambhuva,* the self Existent, and penetrating into the Mundane Egg it emerges from it, at the end of divine incubation, as Brahma, or *Prajapati,* the progenitor of the future Universe, into which he expands. He is *Purusha,* or "Spirit," but is also *Prakriti,* or "Matter". Therefore it is only after separating itself into two halves. *Brahma-Vach* (the female) and *Brahma-Viraj* (the male), that the *Prajapati* becomes the male Brahma.

According to Manu, *Heranyagarbha* is Brahma, the first male formed by the indiscernable "Causeless Cause", in a Golden Egg, resplendant as the Sun, "*Heranyagarbha*" meaning the Golden, or rather the Effulgent Womb or Egg."

The Geometrical derivation of the inspirations which resulted in these sublime imagerys is apparent on every hand.

A significant passage of the *Dyzan Chohans,* or "Stanzas of Dyzan", the archaic Hindoo writing, from which H. P. B. built up the Secret Doctrine, reads as follows, speaking of Maya, the "Great illusion" or Nature, the reflex of Deity—

"Her heart had not yet opened for the One ray to enter, thence to fall, as Three into Four, into the lap of Maya"
The Seven were not yet born from the Web of Light. Darkness alone was Father, Mother Svabhavat and Svabhavat was in Darkness"
"The Three fall into Four. The Radiant Essence becomes Seven inside, Seven outside. The luminous Egg, which in itself is Three (A.U.M.) curdles and spreads in milk white curds throughout the depths of Mother.
The Root that grows out of the depth of the Ocean of Life".

"This was the Army of the Voice (Logos)
The Divine Mother of the Seven.
The Sparks of the Seven are subject to and the servants of the First, the Second, the Third, the Fourth, the Fifth, the Sixth and the Seventh of the Seven.

"These are called Spheres, Triangles, Cubes, Lines and Modellers, for thus stands the eternal Nedana—the Oi-Ha-Hou (Iao or Jod, Heh, Vau, the sum of which is 3 x 7 or 21)

"And these Three, enclosed within the circle are the Sacred Four (The Tetragrammaton?) and the Ten (1—2—3—4) are the Arupa Universe—(26—10—36 the number of the Sun)

Thus were formed the Arupa and the Rupa. From One light, Seven* Lights, from each of the Seven, Seven times Seven Lights (49—21—28=3-4)"

"The Number Seven, according to the Kabbalah," says H. P. B., "is the great number of the Divine Mysteries." Who can fail to discover it in the seven triangles of the geometrical Egg? (Fig. 11.)

"In the *Secret Doctrine*, the figure 4 is the male symbol only on the highest plane of abstraction.

On the plane of Matter, the 3 is the Masculine and the 4 feminine—the upright and the horizontal in the fourth stage of symbolism when the symbols become the glyphs of the generative powers on the physical plane." (The right-angle of 3—4 in the Pythagorean problem, as *Osiris* and *Isis*, Spirit and Matter or God and Nature, Sun and Earth.

Fig. 21. "Three times Three" is 3x3, 3x4 and 3x5 or "Thirty-six", the Pythagorean and consequently "Secret Doctrinal" number of the Solar Logos. An ancient Indian symbol of Deity, often incorrectly drawn.

*The Nebular hypothesis of our Universe.

CPSIA information can be obtained at www.ICGtesting.com
Printed in the USA
BVOW07s0616260314

348824BV00006B/432/P